The Moment of Truth

The Moment of Truth

*Reflections on
Incarnation and Resurrection*

Samuel Wells

CANTERBURY
PRESS
Norwich

First published in 2023 by the Canterbury Press Norwich
Editorial office
3rd Floor, Invicta House
108–114 Golden Lane
London EC1Y 0TG, UK

www.canterburypress.co.uk

Canterbury Press is an imprint of Hymns Ancient & Modern Ltd
(a registered charity)

Hymns Ancient & Modern® is a registered trademark of
Hymns Ancient & Modern Ltd
13A Hellesdon Park Road, Norwich,
Norfolk NR6 5DR, UK

British Library Cataloguing in Publication data

A catalogue record for this book is available
from the British Library

978-1-78622-519-1

Typeset by Regent Typesetting
Printed and bound in Great Britain by
CPI Group (UK) Ltd

For Lucie

Contents

Author's Note

I'm grateful to Anne Gidion and Alexander Deeg for the invitation that gave me the idea for this book, and to members of the 2022 Societas Homiletica gathering in Budapest who reflected with me on the themes it raises.

Like many books, it was written in the company of Jo, Laurie and Steph, together with Harry, Lola, Melita and Rosella, to whose indulgence and shared enjoyment this book is a tribute.

The book is dedicated to Lucie Kitchener – a person of courage and grace, unafraid of the truth.

Introduction:
The Moment of Truth

There's an irony at the heart of liturgically-shaped Christian spirituality. The two central festivals, Christmas and Easter, celebrating the two foundational Christian claims of the incarnation and the resurrection, are so significant that each accords to itself a period of preparation, devotion and reflection: Advent and Lent. There's an ambiguity about both seasons. Advent is traditionally not about Christ's first coming as a baby but about his second coming in judgement and vindication and mercy; but it has inevitably come to be seen as a period of preparation for Christmas. Lent begins as a time of fasting, prayer, resolution, abstinence and simplification; but by its fifth Sunday is thoroughly oriented towards Holy Week and Christ's passion.

But in both cases the faithful congregation arrives at the great day and then – tends to take a break. The First Sundays after Christmas and Easter are described as Low Sundays, the clergy are often on leave, and what might be thought of as the high points of the Christian year are understated and under-observed. In the twentieth century the practice of keeping Advent and Lent came to be marked by the publication of appropriate books reflecting on the respective seasons and the great days that constitute their climaxes. But few books dwell on those great days themselves – as if the faithful need a break from festivity (in the case of Advent) or mortification (in the case of Lent and Holy Week).

Which is why I sensed that a book addressing Christmas and Easter might be appropriate, helpful and timely. I've called it

The Moment of Truth because it is on these two days that the truth of the Christian gospel depends. If Christ is not risen, Paul points out, the Christian faith largely subsides into maudlin identification with suffering and a general sense that we should love our neighbour. If God is not in Christ, as Paul again points out, there is no guarantee that Jesus' words and deeds go beyond those of Socrates, Buddha or Mohammed. By truth I don't mean a medical examination to prove whether there was a virgin birth or a forensic exploration of the first-century tombs surrounding Jerusalem. I refer to what is entailed in the twin claims that Jesus is Emmanuel, God with us, and Jesus is risen, going ahead of us.

Perhaps the most important of the reflections in the first part of the book concerns the question of whether, if there had been no fall, Jesus would still have come. This is a question with a long pedigree in both the Eastern and Western Church. It's one that's become exceptionally important to me. If you answer no, you're looking at a short story that stretches from fall to redemption. If you answer yes, you're looking at a much larger story, beginning before the foundation of the world and stretching to the last day – a story that sees God as being fundamentally committed to be with us, in contrast to the God to whom we look to fix the world for us. In early 2008, while serving as Dean of Duke University Chapel in North Carolina, I made an Ash Wednesday resolution: that I would seek to preach an Easter sermon that did not include the words victory, conquest or triumph. I wanted to explore what it meant to perceive Christ's resurrection as a reaffirmation of what God intended in creation and incarnation – a sense of the world's goodness and of Christ's coming to enjoy the world and not to fix it. It's a resolution I've never gone back on. That commitment has also rolled on into my Christmas preaching. Whereas the traditional Nine Lessons and Carols begins with the fall narrative from Genesis 3.1–6, my Christmas sermons have been flavoured with God's enjoyment of creation and commitment to be with humankind come what may. In the words of the penultimate line of the celebrated hymn 'Be thou my vision',

God says to Israel and to us, 'Heart of my own heart, whatever befall.'

Another reason why I've called the book *The Moment of Truth* is that Christmas and Easter have an abiding resonance in what has, since 1948, become an increasingly secular culture. These are moments when the culture in general is more receptive to a word from Christian leaders and spokespeople, particularly if that word is political, passionate or controversial; and this is an occasion when a husband might join his more faithful spouse, a child his more committed parent, a sibling her more devoted relative at a service of worship, whether from wistfulness, nostalgia, respect or longing. So a sermon at a Christmas or Easter service (and that includes a carol service) does well to pause and highlight the significance and power of what Christianity claims about these two festivals. Truth is a devalued currency in a post-truth 'fake news' era. But I believe by speaking to gut and soul, by dwelling tenderly in the places of visceral fear, hope, despair, terror, joy and desire, the preacher can transcend the weariness and cynicism of our times and re-engage the mind and heart of the listener with urgency and integrity. That is what the reflections in this short volume seek to do.

I have divided the Christmas section into three and the Easter section into two. I should explain why. As to Christmas, I perceive broadly three ways of speaking about the incarnation. The first is to focus in on the narrative itself: this is to look particularly at the Luke story, and to some extent at Matthew's account, and enter into the world of the characters described. For example, Joseph is a fascinating figure: his emotions are only to be imagined, but they must be ones of displacement: displaced from the centre of the story and displaced as the father of Mary's child. But all the characters in the story bear such scrutiny, and it is a fine way to reflect on Christmas. A second approach is to dwell with the customs and absurdities of our contemporary celebration of Christmas: the horror of being without a gift for a close relative, the frenzy of purchasing when invariably a gift, however generous, will not address flaws in the relationship, the palaver of going to one set of in-laws for Christmas and the other for New Year. These are the emotions people bring into church on Christmas Day – and Christmas, more than any other moment, is the occasion for starting where people are. The preacher who speaks to such concerns will find congregation members responding, 'I thought you were talking just to me.' But a third kind of reflection speaks about the incarnation on a much wider canvas – as the intersection of time and eternity, as the moment of forever now, as the meeting of flesh and word. All three have their place, and I trust will be helpful to the reader.

As to Easter, there is a similar distinction between what I perceive as two kinds of reflection. The first focuses on the lyric: the emotions and transformations in the events of the first Easter, most compellingly and thrillingly the meeting of a man and a woman in a garden, and Mary Magdalene's extraordinary realization of who it really was that she was talking to. The second focuses on the epic: the grand sweep of what Easter signifies, existentially, globally, cosmically. Again, both are suitable material for dwelling on the mystery and glory of Easter; and each can be approached from several angles, as I hope my reflections show.

The final reason I have named this book *The Moment of Truth* is that truth is seriously out of fashion, even amongst those who believe and faithfully walk the Christian way. It's out of fashion because Christians have become so beleaguered by those who have much to gain from deriding the faith, from outside and sometimes from within, that many have planted their flag on something other than truth, like usefulness or comfort. It's out of fashion because those who shout loudly about truth have acquired a reputation for intolerance, either of different expressions of faith, or of diverse human identities, or of other faith traditions – and not wanting to be thought small-minded, more generous Christians have stepped aside from the word truth. It's out of fashion because we live in an era where truth has been something one can question, discredit or undermine by throwing over it claims of bias, misrepresentation, vested interest or privilege; and to avoid the grief of such controversies, it sometimes seems better to avoid the word entirely. Which is why I landed on the phrase 'the moment of truth'. May this book be such a moment for those who read it – a moment squirrelled away from the pressure to avoid the questions the book addresses, a moment of confronting the biggest claims Christianity makes, a moment of no longer delaying, doubting or dispelling the biggest issues of all, but sitting with them with an open mind and a tender heart.

PART I

Christmas

I

Laid in a Manger:
Reflections on the Nativity

But...

The story is told of a British preacher who went to visit the United States. She'd prepared a careful three-point sermon on the subject of the word 'But'. No one had told her that in America 'butt' means 'backside'. And so she embarked on the first point of her sermon: 'Everyone has a but'. She was a little bit confused by the congregation's response. Undeterred, she carried on to her second point, 'You can see other people's buts'. Now the congregation didn't seem to be getting her argument, but there was nothing to be done but to carry on to her third and most significant point, 'But you can't see your own but'.

The story of Christmas is one in which almost every character has a 'but'. It starts with Zechariah. Zechariah was a priest of the Temple in Jerusalem. There were so many priests that each group only got to serve for two weeks a year, and when a group was performing the morning and evening sacrifices, they would draw lots for which of their number would also make the incense offerings. Zechariah's name was drawn, and in he went to the sanctuary. There he met Gabriel, the angel of the Lord, who announced that he, Zechariah, would have a son named John, who would make ready a people prepared for the Lord. The way Luke tells the story, it reminds us of Abraham and Elkanah, two old men in the Old Testament who had sons according to God's promise, Isaac and Samuel. But it turns out Zechariah has a very big 'but': 'But I'm too old'. Zechariah's 'but' is that he can't believe God still has a use for an old man like him.

The next character is Joseph. Just as in Luke's account an angel appeared to Zechariah, so in Matthew's account an angel appears to Joseph. Joseph knew that he was of the lineage of David, the family from whom the messiah was expected to come. He also knew his fiancée was pregnant. What he found a little difficult to believe was that the father of the child was the Holy Spirit. Like a lot of people, Joseph was more than a little concerned with the gossip in the village, at the shops, in the offices, on the workshop floor. It's not a nice situation to be in, to be planning to marry a young woman and suddenly to discover that she is expecting a baby, and to know the baby isn't yours. Joseph is a kind and good man and doesn't get angry or humiliate Mary. Which of us would have been as generous as he was? But Joseph was nevertheless a man with a very big 'but'. 'But what will people say?' He could square it in his own imagination, but he struggled to see how others would do so.

Then we move to a third character, who doesn't appear in the scriptural story but who has become the stuff of every nativity play performed ever since. I refer to the innkeeper. Luke gives us a simple line 'she laid him in a manger, because there was no place for them at the inn'. Out of this line we have created endless sequences of grumpy innkeepers, menageries of farm animals, beds of straw and little donkeys. But the innkeeper, fictional or not, is a man we can all relate to. He is forever remembered as a man who was so preoccupied with the cares of his world that he had no room for Jesus. He is a man with a big but: 'But I'm too busy.'

And then there are the wise men. They are sages, magi, astrologers. They have been consulting the skies for a long time. They have a deep understanding of the mysteries of the universe. They have discovered a special star, a star that heralds the birth of a new king, a king whose influence matters not just on earth but also in heaven. They travel afar, bearing gifts. But then they face a crisis of faith and wisdom. They assume that the king of the Jews must be born in Jerusalem. These are very clever, very courageous and very patient men. But they have a big but: 'But the Son of God can't be born in a stable in a small insignificant town.'

So here are four characters from the Christmas story: four characters who each have a big but: but I'm too old, but what will people say, but I'm too busy, but this isn't the God I'd expected.

There are other characters who see things differently. One is Elizabeth. Elizabeth was Zechariah's wife. She was past her best-before date. Her hopes of having a child seemed to be over. She could have said, 'But I'm too old'. Yet it seems she didn't. Instead, she said, 'This is what the Lord has done for me by looking favourably on me.'

Another character is Mary. This must have been a terrifying time for her. Having a child is a daunting prospect at the best of times, but just imagine being a young girl swept up into God's destiny and facing the misunderstanding of your whole community. Mary could have had lots of big buts: 'But I'm too young', 'But I'm too scared', 'But why me?' We can hardly blame her for saying, 'But I'm a virgin.' But Mary left all the buts to one side, and when Gabriel told her what God had in store she simply responded, 'Here am I, the servant of the Lord.'

Finally, there are the shepherds. Of all the characters in the story, these might have had the biggest reason to find a big but. The life of a shepherd was a hard one. Not only did they spend most of their life far from the comforts and company of home; even worse, the fact that they were incapable of keeping the ritual and dietary standards of the Jewish law meant that they were regarded as unclean and therefore outside God's favour. Alone of all the characters in the Christmas story, they have not the slightest hint of a but. They don't say 'But we are only shepherds.' All they say is, 'Let us go now and see this thing that has taken place.' They put their livelihoods in danger by leaving their sheep in the field, and they put what little reputation they had in jeopardy by telling the whole community what they had heard and seen. For the shepherds, there is no but: simply celebration and thanksgiving.

As we look at our lives on Christmas Day, and take away the wrapping paper of nostalgia and sentimentality, the question for us is, where do we fit into this story? Do we have a big but – but I'm too old, but what will people say, but I'm too busy, but this isn't the God I expected, but how can this be? Or are we like the shepherds, a little scared but eager to respond to whatever new thing God has in store?

The heart of Christmas is the word Emmanuel, God with us. The good news of the Christmas story is that God found a way to be with us, despite our buts. God found a way to be with Zechariah by giving him a hopeful wife. God found a way to be with Joseph by speaking to him in a dream. God found a way to be with the innkeeper by coming in the back door. God found a way to be with the wise men by sending them scurrying back to their books of prophecy. God finds a way to be with us whether we say 'But ... but ... but' or not. That is the good news of Christmas. And the good news of Christmas is good news for today. For God shall be with us until all buts have ceased and we behold each other face to face.

What changes – and what doesn't

The Christmas story in Luke's gospel comes in two parts. The first part tells us what's wrong with the world. The second part tells us how God longs for things to be. Studying the Christmas story can, I think, help us as we try to discern what changes because of Jesus, and what doesn't.

How things are

The first part of the story begins, 'In those days a decree went out from Emperor Augustus that all the world should be registered.' This sentence tells us most of what we need to know about what's wrong with the world. It tells us that someone is in charge, and able to issue decrees, and that that person is not

God. It tells us that that person is able to send his decrees to the whole world. Of course the whole world as it appeared to Luke is a little smaller than the whole world as we understand it today; but the point is that the emperor ruled everything he knew about, and if he'd known about India and Sub-Saharan Africa and America and China he'd have made pretty sure he was ruling over those places too. The emperor is God. That's what this opening sentence is telling us. The emperor is known as the Son of God, the bringer of peace, the Lord, the saviour of the world – in fact, everything the angels later say about Jesus the Romans were accustomed to saying about Augustus. After all, he had brought to an end a generation of civil war in the Roman Empire. There was plenty to celebrate. Not maybe in Palestine, but certainly in Rome.

And what Augustus' decree said is that everyone needed to be registered. Now this isn't a simple matter of wanting to know how big his empire was – like a mega-church wanting to know how many people come through its doors or eBay wanting to know how many people visit its website in the run-up to Christmas. No, it's a little more sinister than that. No registration without taxation. This is about money. Having the Roman Empire ruling over you wasn't a privilege you got for free; you had to pay for it. And Rome wasn't terribly interested in the territories it invaded for their own sake: it was only interested in what it could get out of them. We get a hint of this when Luke tells us that this registration was 'while Quirinius was governor of Syria' – that's to say, at this point in history Israel only figured on Augustus' map as a subdivision of the province of Syria. Pretty small fry, in other words.

Luke's views about taxation become clear much later in the story. When Jesus stands before Pilate, one of the principal accusations against him is that he was forbidding Jews to pay taxes to Caesar. A little earlier, Jesus is asked whether it is lawful to pay taxes to Caesar. Jesus responds by picking up a coin. He points out that the head on the coin is that of the Emperor. You need to remember that there weren't any newspapers or radio or television in these times. Coins were the major form of propaganda. Jesus says, in as many words, 'If you want to worship the emperor, that's up to you. But don't forget everything in the end belongs to God.' The point is that taxation wasn't just a means of raising money. It was also a way of humiliating subject peoples. It's worth remembering that the people asking Jesus the question about taxes and later making the accusations against him were the chief priests, who themselves also taxed the Jewish people and held together the whole system of taxation. So what Luke is saying in the opening words of the Christmas story is, 'Look at what things had come to: Augustus was ordering the affairs of Israel just as God was supposed to do, and the leaders of Israel were following the instructions of Augustus in just the way that they should have been following the instructions of God.'

Luke is assuming his readers know the story of Israel well. And the story of Israel doesn't just disclose the general principle that all things belong to God. It also offers a specific example on the subject of a census. In 2 Samuel 24 King David takes a census of the people of Israel and Judah. We aren't told exactly why this was considered a terrible sin, but we have to assume it was one of a number of ways in which David treated Israel as his possession to dispose of how he wished, rather than as God's gift to be cherished and fostered. David accepts that he has sinned, and gets to choose his punishment; interestingly, he says to God, 'Let us fall into the hands of the Lord, for his mercy is great; but let me not fall into human hands.' Which brings us back to the census taken by Emperor Augustus, because it demonstrates beyond doubt that Israel has fallen into human hands, whose mercy is not great.

So the first thing wrong with the world is that it is in the grip of oppressive forces, and in this story the emperor Augustus is the overwhelming force that not only takes away the people's freedom but imposes himself as their new god. And into this story comes a descendant of David, to be born in the city of David. The most curious thing about the Christmas story in Luke is that Luke gives us five verses about a census, twelve verses about shepherds and angels, and only two verses about the birth itself.

And what we discover in those two verses about the birth itself is the second thing that is wrong with the world. This second thing is that it has no place for Jesus. The conventional Christmas nativity play has Joseph and Mary arriving in Bethlehem late at night, with Mary already feeling labour pains, reaching for the gas and air, and wondering why the epidural hasn't been invented yet. Then we see Joseph going from innkeeper to innkeeper, pleading for mercy for his belaboured wife and being told that because of the census every motel is booked up for miles around. At last one of the innkeepers has a heart and puts them in the stable. But little or nothing of this is in Luke's story. It's all our embellishment. What Luke tells us is that Joseph and Mary went to Bethlehem. It doesn't tell us that Bethlehem was heaving with business. It doesn't say that Mary was already deep into her third trimester. She and Joseph may well have been in Bethlehem for a while. Luke just says, 'While they were there, the time came for her to deliver her child.' Luke takes the time to point out that this was her firstborn son. In other words, as for many women in those days and even today, this was the most profound moment of her entire life, the moment when she gave birth to her first child. And what kind of hospitality did she get, in the city of her husband's ancestors? Zilch. The child went in the animals' feeding trough. Can you imagine how many health and safety checks that feeding trough would have failed? This is putting the most vulnerable person in Bethlehem in the most dangerous place in the whole town.

And what the story is saying, of course, is that God's chosen people, the faithful of the time, just like the faithful today, weren't ready, weren't interested, weren't looking for the coming of God. If you imagine the symbolism of the scene, this was a house in which the animals lived downstairs, providing the heat for the humans who lived upstairs. So the fact that Jesus was born downstairs and laid in the animals' feeding trough is a vivid depiction of what the incarnation enacts: God came down from heaven and took earthly, fleshly form, while the people for whom he came were largely oblivious to what was going on. In St John's words, 'He was in the world, yet the world did not know him' (John 1.10). In fact, he was in the *house*, and the people in the *house* didn't know him.

So that just about sums up what was wrong with the world, and what's wrong with the world today. The world is in the grip of oppressive forces; and meanwhile those who profess to open their lives to Jesus aren't interested or paying attention when the moment of truth comes along.

Let's look now at the second part of the story, the part about the shepherds and the angels. 'Shepherd' is of course a very familiar word in the biblical vocabulary. It particularly reminds us of two Old Testament books. The first is Ezekiel, which denounces the leaders of Israel prior to the Exile as false shepherds, leading the flock of their people astray. The second is the Psalms, where we are told 'The Lord is my shepherd. I shall not want.' These two references make it clear that shepherds, far from being marginal people excluded from the dietary laws on which the Pharisees insisted and therefore ritually unclean, are instead at the heart of the symbolic world of the gospel. They epitomize everything that was wrong in Israel and everything that God wishes to set right. And of course David was a shepherd boy before he became king. And it is in the new David, the Christ child, that God will become once again the shepherd of Israel.

But there is one rather subtler aspect of the shepherds' significance. Shepherds are people who keep sheep. Sheep were kept in ancient Israel not just for food and for wool but for sacrifice. Bethlehem is just a few miles from Jerusalem. It's not too fanciful to suppose that these lambs were being reared for Temple sacrifices. Remember that every household had to sacrifice a lamb in the Temple at Passover. That's a lot of lambs. And yet Jesus isn't born in the Temple. He's the Lamb of God but he's born with the animals, not with their slayers. So here again Jesus' birth echoes the problem of Israel – the Temple sacrifice system that did not take away sin, while at the same time hinting at the solution – the Lamb of God, the new shepherd who was to be what the Temple always promised to be: the definitive place of encounter between God and Israel.

In many ways the heart of the story lies in what the shepherds learn from the angels. The first thing they learn is that
what's happening is fundamentally about joy. The registration
that took Joseph and Mary to Bethlehem was about taxation,
oppression, humiliation. But this is about joy. Then they learn
that this is joy for all people. The story of the census began with
all the world, the world that was under Caesar's thumb: but
this is good news of great joy for all people. In other words, for
everyone under oppression, hear the news of fabulous joy. The
angels mention David again, for the third time in ten verses,
just to make sure you don't miss that this is about David, who
was himself a shepherd like these shepherds and became a king
like Jesus, who himself had a census like Augustus and yet came
to realize that all things and all people belong to God. Then
the shepherds learn that this child is to be Saviour, Messiah
and Lord, bringing glory and peace – in other words he is to
be all that Augustus claims to be and more. He's bigger than
Rome and he's the fulfilment of the longings of Israel. All things
earthly and heavenly. And then the surprise – he's plonked in
an animal feeding trough. In other words, he's already been
subject to the oppression of Rome that has dragged his parents
a hundred miles on foot back to Bethlehem and he's already suf-
fered rejection by his people and got tossed in the hay instead of
being given a decent place to lay his head.

And then – pow! A whole army of angels appears in the heavens. The language we're used to, 'a multitude of the heavenly
host', again obscures the significance of these words. Behind the
angel appears a whole *battalion* of angels. The name Gabriel
means 'God is my warrior'. This is military imagery. What
this is telling the shepherds is, 'Don't worry, God can kick the
Romans out of Palestine any time it suits – just look at the
armies God's got to call on. But these armies gathered not for
warfare but for worship, because this baby embodies everything
God is about.'

And what happens when the angels leave is that the shepherds become angels. Angels are, after all, messengers. And the
shepherds become messengers, amazing people with what they

have to tell them and returning to their sheep glorifying God for all they had heard and seen. And as the story ends, with the shepherds glorifying God, we remember how Luke's whole gospel ends, with the eleven disciples returning from Bethany with great joy and glorifying God. And we realize how this Christmas story is a microcosm of the whole gospel story, beginning with Rome's oppression and Israel's rejection, and ending with a new set of shepherds (the disciples) who themselves turn into angelic messengers (or apostles).

By the end of the story some things have changed, and some haven't. What *hasn't* changed is this: there's still oppression in the world, and even the faithful still have little or no room for Jesus when he's looking for a place to stay. But what *has* changed is this: God has entered the story, definitively, vulnerably and permanently, with the power to overturn the oppressor and confront the hard-hearted. But God chooses to be made known as a tiny baby who needs and desires our loving and longing response. And the first people to learn of God's coming are shepherds, whose work is sometimes ordinary, sometimes excluded, sometimes humiliating. And the good news of God's coming turns those shepherds, as it turns us, into angels who have seen the glory of God, have wonders to tell, and whose hearts are full of joy. That's the good news of Christmas.

Christmas is about what matters

I got a call from a journalist around the second week of October. I guess it was a slow news week, so she'd tried everyone else and thought she'd get a story out of me. She said, 'Did you see the Christmas decorations are up on Oxford Street already?' I said, 'How 'bout that.' She said, 'Don't you think everything's all getting so commercial?' I said, 'You know, I've been visiting Oxford Street for quite a while, and it's been pretty commercial all that time, so far as I can recall.' She said, 'But Christmas – don't you think it's all got so commercial?' I said, 'Well people have got to make a living, and this is the time of year customers like to buy things. As a matter of fact, we have a business here at St Martin's, and we do about a third of our turnover in the last couple of months of the year too. If the storekeepers want to spruce up the street by putting some sparkly tinsel and twinkly lights outside, I think that's rather nice.'

My journalist wasn't going to be deterred. She said, 'But don't you think it's confusing for people? With Harvest just done and Hallowe'en and Guy Fawkes coming up – they get all these festivals mixed up.' I said, 'I'd give people a bit more credit than that. Most folk I know are pretty intelligent. They know an angel on a tree from a witch on a broom; they know a firework from a harvest loaf; they know a bonfire from a Christingle candle.'

At this stage I began to get a sense of what was going on. I said, 'Are you calling because you want me to be angry and denounce people going to parties and buying presents?' And then I felt a wave of sadness and shame sweep over me, for my church and for its clergy. How had we got ourselves a reputation for being against people celebrating Christmas, enjoying each other and giving each other gifts? How had we created a situation where a journalist thought she could get an easy story by telling a vicar there were lights on Oxford Street and then sitting back and waiting for a feast of denunciation? So I said, 'Actually I'm really happy that people are out spending their money on showing other people how much they love them. I think that's rather beautiful.'

But she hadn't finished. She got out what was clearly her trump card. 'Don't you think the problem is,' she said conclusively, 'that Christmas has just got so materialistic?' I was silent. She said, 'Are you still there?' I said, 'Yes, I'm still here. But I need to tell you you've got that one completely wrong. Christmas is the celebration that God became material. At Christmas we remember just how God took material form inside the womb of Mary, God was wrapped in the material of swaddling clothes when Jesus was laid in a manger, God was put at material risk when Herod killed all the babies in Bethlehem looking for the new-born king. Christmas is about materialism. That's exactly what we're celebrating. Christmas is about the God who made the material world at creation becoming part of the material world in Jesus. You can't get more materialistic than God. It's impossible.'

At that point the journalist realized she didn't have a story and we called it a day. But if she'd wanted to hear more, this is what I'd have told her. The old-fashioned phrase, 'That's not material' is a way of saying, 'That doesn't matter.' The words material and matter come from the same root. They're about substance, as in the phrase 'vegetable matter', and about importance, as in the famous song lyric, 'nothing really matters to me.'

The Christmas story is about what really matters. It turns out that almost every detail in the story is about something easily ignored or people who're habitually told they don't matter. The story begins with the shabbiness of a woman pregnant with a baby her husband-to-be hasn't fathered. Women with no economic independence or social standing matter. Then there's a census that drags people back to their father's home town, leaving Mary and Joseph with no bed for the night. Homeless people matter. Then they have their baby and lay him in an animal feeding trough. All of God's creatures matter. The new family get their first visit from social outcasts, shepherds, who're despised because they can't keep the ritual washing regulations. Socially excluded, dirty, rough, despised people matter. Then they get a visit from some foreigners, travellers of another faith. People of other races and religions matter. Then the little family escapes to Egypt because Herod wants to kill the little boy. Oppressed people and refugees matter.

In the last 200 years our culture has turned Christmas into a season of bonhomie and the idealization of the nuclear family. But the Christmas story is telling us what matters: women with no status, migrants and homeless people, the non-human creation, social outcasts, foreigners, people of other religions, oppressed people and refugees. It's not that we should spare a thought at Christmas for disadvantaged people: they're what the Christmas story is all about, they take all the main parts, they're centre stage. *They're what matters.* Of course we sentimentalize the Christmas story to be about a little donkey, a dusty road, a lullaby and a baby who lays down his sweet head. But that's because we struggle so much with who the story is really about, and what the story is really saying. We want it to be a sweet story about long ago. It turns out it's a very challenging story about today.

What else matters at Christmas? God matters. All the angels in the sky and stars in the heavens, decisions of emperors and movements of peoples – they're the backdrop for what's really going on. What's really going on is expressed in the angel's word, Emmanuel: God is with us. The whole of the Old Testament is about God wanting to be with us: creating Adam and Eve to be companions, making a promise with Noah to be faithful to us, pledging to Abraham to be with his people forever, making a covenant with Moses and then with David to be their people's God always. Finally, in the Christmas story God turns that promise of companionship into flesh and blood. God becomes material. God no longer makes a material covenant in a rainbow or in a tablet of stone or something else: God *becomes* that covenant in the flesh and blood of Jesus. Jesus is the place where God's divinity and our humanity meet. God becomes material. That's why it's so silly to say Christmas has become materialistic. It always was. It's always been all about God becoming material. God becomes substance – matter. God … matters.

But this leaves us with one last thing that matters at Christmas. We've just seen that God matters. But Jesus is not just God. That may seem a bizarre thing to say – how can there be anything more amazing than to say Jesus is God? Well, there is something just as amazing. Jesus is not just God. Jesus is also human. Jesus takes on the flesh of a weak, fragile, clumsy, vulnerable baby. What that's saying is that human beings matter. Human flesh matters. We're not just spiritual beings imprisoned or contained in a physical body. Our physical existence, our material reality, our earthly life really matters. Not just now, but forever. Jesus came to be with us in time so that we might come to be with God in eternity.

There's a deep, terrifying, lonely question inside almost every one of us, which we seldom name and never share. And this is the question: do I matter? Do I matter to anyone? Do I matter for a while – or do I in any sense matter forever? What makes us never ask the question is the fear that the answer is, finally, no. But behold the wonder of Christmas. This is precisely why Christmas matters. At Christmas God makes the people who generally don't matter the centre of the story. At Christmas God becomes just like you and me because what matters to God is being with us always. And at Christmas God is speaking to each one of us, as gently, unthreateningly, passionately and disarmingly as we can possibly imagine.

And what God is saying, through taking the material of our life, are the words that matter more than any we'll ever hear: 'You matter. You matter right now. You matter forever. You matter to me.'

God in our hands

There's nothing more mysterious than the wonder of conception, the gradual shaping of a baby in the womb, and then the agony and ecstasy of birth. Even when you've got a sense of some of the biology behind it, the wonder only increases. The beginnings are tiny. The connections are intricate. The inception is fragile. The development is miraculous. The weaving-together of unique and delicate elements of life is awe-inspiring. On this precarious thread hangs the existence of each one of us.

Birth takes place when the baby's strong enough to live outside the womb, but small enough to make its escape. It's an astonishing, sometimes harrowing, almost always dumbfounding experience. Just look at those tiny toes, that scrunched up nose. But it's still early days. The baby can't feed itself for years, can't wash its own clothes until its thirties, and isn't financially independent until its fifties.

I want to stay with the vulnerability of the new-born baby. One day in 2008, in the Argentine city of Misiones 600 miles north of Buenos Aires, a baby boy was found in the gutter on a city street, surrounded by eight wild cats. The cats were licking him because he was so dirty. They snuggled up with him during freezing nights and saved him from hypothermia. They foraged scraps and kept him alive.

In 2019 in the Russian city of Magnitogorsk, 900 miles southeast of Moscow, a block of flats collapsed following a gas explosion. Rescuers searched amid the debris in temperatures as low as -20C. Frequently they had to halt their search while workers tried to remove or stabilize sections of the building in danger of collapse. Eventually, after 35 hours of searching, they heard cries. They found a tiny baby boy and pulled him from the rubble. The regional governor then said an extraordinary thing. 'The child was saved because it was in a crib and wrapped warmly.'

I want to suggest to you that these two stories show us vital dimensions of the Christmas story. The first one, from Argentina, with the eight cats and the baby in the gutter, is a modern-day manger scene: a tiny child surrounded by animals, facing the cold shoulder of a dangerous world. The second one, from Russia, with the patient rescuers and the rubble and the crying baby, is about a more pressing danger – more like King Herod's determination to slaughter all the new-born boys in Bethlehem; a danger from which the baby Jesus so narrowly escaped.

These two modern-day stories, with their vivid portrayal of the vulnerability and the fragility of a helpless baby, give us a remarkable insight into the unique wonder of Christianity. Let's take that wonder in three stages. The first is the most familiar. It's what we call the incarnation. God's desire to be our companion was so deep that it involved coming among us as a human being. It meant growing up in a carpenter's home, sharing the village dramas and struggles of Nazareth, facing the challenge and tension of ministry in Galilee, and eventually enduring the betrayal and agony of death in Jerusalem. That's wonder enough.

But look at the stage beyond that: being a tiny, defenceless baby. If Jesus were simply a superhuman hero, why would he need to undergo the trauma of birth at all? It's said to be the worst experience we ever go through, being born. You'd think he could just show up in Galilee, fully grown, good to go. But God becomes flesh as the most vulnerable little person imaginable, at the mercy of inexperienced parents, clumsy animals, dangerous buildings, hostile rulers. How vulnerable can you get?

And this brings us to the third most awesome dimension. There's a hundred ways it could all have gone wrong. If this was a masterplan to fix the world and set everything right, you've got to say the risk register's full to bursting. What makes the Argentine wild cats and the Russian rubble stories so amazing is that 999 times out of a thousand those stories end a different way. The baby dies. The baby's got no chance being looked after by wild cats; even less chance being found alive after 35 hours with no food in below freezing temperatures. Yet the Christmas story is just as scary: born amid animals, pursued almost immediately by a ruthless tyrant. No chance. It's a miracle he reached the age of one.

We love the donkey, the dusty road, the angels, the shepherds in tea towels, the wise men bringing Turkish Delight containers. We love all the details of the Christmas story. But this part, even the most devoted believer shies away from. Because for all our fury with God's apparent inaction in the face of building collapse, abandoned children or global pandemic, we still picture God as elderly, wise, bearded, white-robed, a bit gruff, and stuck to a gilded ceiling. And what the Christmas story shows us is a God who is none of those things. All the things we thought we distrusted or dismissed about God – they all fall away at this moment.

We say, 'I hate the fact that you can control everything, but you still let bad things happen.' God says, 'I'm a helpless baby before your eyes.' We say, 'I hate the way you're so powerful and mighty and you justify all the ways power and privilege and force dominate the world and dictate who can thrive and who will suffer.' God says, 'I'm a tiny infant, as vulnerable to rejection and hatred and neglect as you are.' We say, 'I hate all the chances I've missed and the odds stacked against me and how my life's never going to come right or be happy.' God says,

'Here I am, I'm a child in your arms. The future of everything is in your hands.'

We depict ourselves as weak, vulnerable and helpless – and we project on to God all our anger, frustration and resentment. But God appears as this fragile, utterly defenceless baby – and all our arguments melt away. What if this is what God really looks like? What if God is so longing to be in relationship with us that the central image of that relationship is of God longing to be embraced by us, made warm by us, cradled by us? So much so that, if we don't respond, the whole future of everything, the whole destiny of God, is in jeopardy.

We're not sure we really want that. We're not quite sure we're really ready to have God in our hands. We're not entirely confident we're really ready for Christmas. We'd actually prefer the superman-rescuer Jesus after all. Well, it's time to discover the real Christmas. Maybe for the very first time. God risks absolutely everything to be cradled in our arms. God is entrusted to us. Big enough to make the whole universe. Small enough to fit in our embrace. That's the wonder of Christmas. We've got the destiny of the universe in our hands.

Under the radar

When I was 19 I decided to make a trip to the land of my birth, Canada, to meet some relatives and find out whether I had any affinity with the country I'd not seen since I was a baby. En route I got to meet a variety of what A. A. Milne would call 'Rabbit's friends and relations'. In Washington D.C., I found Cousin Jim, my father's cousin, who was known in the family for one thing only: he claimed to have invented radar. We sat down to dinner and his wife made the opening gambit: 'Your father,' she said, 'is the *only* one of the Wells relations who has *never* sent us a Christmas card.' It was a frosty beginning. Eventually I managed to turn the conversation round to Cousin Jim's finest hour. 'It all happened,' he said, settling into a tale he'd clearly told a thousand times, 'when I was stationed in the eastern Mediterranean, off Alexandria' – although he said 'the eastern Med' like sailors do with clipped accents in sweaty World War Two films when they call the Germans 'Jerry'.

I later found that there are large numbers of people who claim to have invented radar. But Jim was in no doubt the credit rightly lay with him. Finishing his story, in the manner of a military memoir, he said, 'If I have one regret, I never worked out how to get between the mountains to stop those beastly bombers flying under the radar. Still – always good to leave something for your successors to finish off' – and he looked up at a 45-degree angle like American presidents do, as if anticipating the acclaim of posterity.

To understand the Christmas story, we need to grasp two dimensions that are apparently contradictory but on closer scrutiny are both showing us the same thing. The first is what we could call the wide-angle version, the second the close-up picture. Let's start with the wide angle.

The universe is impossibly large to imagine, stretching to trillions of stars; and who knows if there are plenty of other universes beyond this one. But that which lasts forever, which we know as God, seems to have a particular interest in this tiny planet in this obscure galaxy. It seems useless to speculate why this planet, in this galaxy, in this universe – the point is, that which lasts forever seems to have so ordered things as to be in relationship with one part of creation – in short, us. The whole epic magnitude of existence has come about in order for God to be among us as one of us and to be our companion and dwell with us. That's the wide-angle version of Christmas. It answers the perennial question, 'What's the meaning of life?' The answer is, the meaning of life is for God to be in relationship with us and for us to reflect the joy and glory of that relationship by relating to one another and the wider creation in the same way. That's the meaning of Christmas – the wide-angle version.

And so to the close-up picture. The three accounts of the coming of Christ, in Matthew, Luke and John's gospels, are significantly different from one another. But they all agree on one thing. Matthew talks about a man called Joseph who discovers his fiancée is expecting a baby and is told by an angel that the Holy Spirit has brought this about. Luke sees it from Mary's point of view and locates the conversation in Nazareth. Luke adds the story about the census and there being no room at the inn, and tells us about the shepherds and angels. John misses out the personal detail and describes how the animating force in the universe became a human being: but interestingly he adds this sentence, which we seldom talk about at Christmas but which seems to me very significant: 'He was in the world, and the world came into being through him; yet the world did not know him.'

What these three contrasting accounts have in common is that the entry of the creator of all things into the human drama didn't happen in the way we might expect. It happened in an obscure backwater of the Roman Empire. It the happened to an ordinary woman and a bewildered man with no social prominence. It happened in a shed. It was witnessed by lowly herdsmen.

Which is why I was put in mind of that conversation with my cousin Jim nearly 40 years ago. What Jim regarded as his oversight was in fact the heart of God's technique: under the radar. Jesus enters creation's story under the radar. He's hardly noticed.

Now you may say this was a foolish, flawed, failed way for God to come among us. Why on earth wasn't there maximum publicity, with words written in the sky above every dwelling the world over? Why wasn't there a voice from heaven, in God's unmistakable Californian accent, speaking slowly like God always does, as if God's always dealing with a dodgy sound system, saying, 'Wake up everybody. This is the biggest moment of all time. Don't miss it.'

Well, this close-up picture takes us to the heart of Christmas. Because yes, God *would* have needed the writing in the sky and the booming voice if the point was to impress people, or to intimidate them, or to dominate the headlines, or to shake people into paying attention. But it turns out that none of these were the reason why God came among us. God came among us to heal our hearts. That can't be done by fireworks or loud voices or great drama or cosmic spectacle.

I discovered what God was up to some while ago when I got to know a woman and a man who told me they wanted to get married. It was a difficult situation. The man had been married before and for a long time had been partly estranged from his wife. The woman was much younger than the man, and from the very start of their relationship felt she had to tiptoe around her family because it was clear they didn't approve. To be fair, she'd spent her whole life tiptoeing, because her family had been a scene of constant wrangling and great pain almost since she'd been born, and she couldn't see why her finally finding happiness was taken so badly by a group of people many of whom it seemed had never found the way to any happiness of their own. But then she became pregnant, and those who disapproved, or took offence or just couldn't bear the idea of someone in the family being happy, all decided this was the moment to say the whole thing was terrible and everyone should be ashamed and what did they think they were doing. But they all turned up to the wedding, and when the bride walked down the aisle, her elegant simplicity, her utterly unpretentious grace, took the wind out of the whole congregation and all misgivings were set aside for the day. Two months later, she gave birth. And she wrote to me and said, 'You'll never guess what's happened. My family has been visiting and have been very kind to everyone including my husband. It's as if this tiny child heals something inside them when they are with him, and their troubles vastly reduce or disappear around him. It made me think of the wonder of God. This little baby has achieved what my husband and I tried to achieve and couldn't over many years. And so effortlessly!' Those were her exact words.

It was one of the most moving messages I've ever received. And not just because this new child had changed the whole dynamic of two troubled families. But because in 70 words this new mother had shown me what God is doing in coming among us as a baby. God is doing just what this baby was doing: something no argument, no loud voice, no lit-up sky, no heavenly vision could achieve. It's called a dismantling of the heart. A disarming of resistance.

God comes to us at Christmas not to blast us into submission, not to make us guilty for what we've got wrong, not to stir us to take up cudgels in the latest battle. God comes to us under the radar. God surprises us by appearing as a tiny baby. It's a high-risk strategy. It's such a vulnerable way to come among us. But it shows us unmistakably, irrevocably, eternally, who God is and what kind of relationship God wants to have with us. God doesn't want us to worry about the wide-angle story our imaginations can't encompass anyway. God says, 'Receive me as you receive this tiny child. Allow me to dismantle centuries of enmity, heal decades of hurt, transform depths of antagonism. Be mesmerized by me the way you're captivated by a tiny baby. Let me melt your heart. So effortlessly.'

What Christmas is really about

For lovers of the Christmas story, I've got news for you. A lot of it isn't in the Bible. For a start there's no little donkey. No dusty road. There are no camels. The people who come across the desert aren't kings, but philosophers or sages. There's no mention of the ox, the ass, or any other animals. It's not certain anyone was wearing a tea towel on their head. It doesn't say the shepherds brought a baby lamb to give to the baby Jesus. There's no account of Mary and Joseph knocking on the door of the first innkeeper and the second innkeeper before finally finding a more accommodating third. It's all embellishment.

Of course, it's harmless. And a lot of it's quite plausible, apart from the tea towels. But it's not completely harmless. Because what's added in as extra colour tends to distract from what is actually there and really matters.

Here's what's in the story. Mary is pregnant. She's looking down the barrel of being disowned by her family and cast aside by her fiancé. She's in a nightmarish financial situation and is moments away from being on the streets, fending for herself.

Joseph and Mary are in Bethlehem. They just washed up there. There's no accommodation. There's no local authority with statutory provision for pregnant women. Mary's moments away from the horrendous risk of giving birth in the open air with no medical attention whatsoever.

The shepherds sleep outside most nights of the week. There are no convenient hostels with showers and washing machines. They look and smell and live like people who have to make do on what they can forage and have no prospect of a wash or shave from one week to the next.

The magi are overseas migrants. There are no hotels in those days. No one's really going to believe a cock and bull story about a star and a new-born king, and their story about crossing the desert to greet a new king doesn't go down at all well in Herod's court. Doesn't matter how posh the magi are, they're out on their ear.

Herod throws his toys out of the pram and suddenly the Holy Family are on the move again, scarpering to Egypt (again, no donkey mentioned) where they are what today we'd call asylum-seekers and seem to have been accepted as refugees.

In other words, what we call the Christmas Story could better be described as the Homeless Story. Everyone's making a journey. But everyone at some stage of the story is homeless. The connection between Christmas and homelessness is not that Christmas is about having a big meal and a bit of a tipple and sharing presents with friends and family and we should spare a thought for the less fortunate. No, that's not the point. The point is that the Christmas Story is about homelessness front, back and sideways. There's scarcely a detail in the whole thing that's not about homelessness. Practically every single character besides Herod is homeless, and even he doesn't really belong and fears being turfed out at any moment. Which is why he's so insecure.

And the theological point of all this is that Christmas is fundamentally about God coming to make a home with us, in order that we might finally and ultimately come to make our home with God. God becomes homeless so that we, wandering, searching, lost, might at long last find our way home. That's what the whole story is really about.

So the best way to spend Christmas is with homeless people.

Not because we sentimentally think that the odd mince pie and well-wrapped thermal vest is really going to change anyone's life. But because homeless people are the heart of the Christmas story and through them we discover and recognize our own true homelessness. And realize, perhaps for the first time, what Christmas is really about.

Showing up

At 9.15 on the morning of 21 October 1966, a colliery spoil tip on a mountain slope above the Welsh village of Aberfan, near Merthyr Tydfil, catastrophically collapsed. It suddenly slid downhill as a slurry, engulfing the local junior school, killing 116 children and 28 adults.

The event occupies an episode in the third series of the Netflix drama, *The Crown*. The episode portrays Queen Elizabeth's uncertainty about how to respond to the disaster. Urged to visit by the Prime Minister, Harold Wilson, she initially states, 'The Crown doesn't do disaster sites; we do hospitals.' She thinks her presence would be a distraction amid the chaos of rescue, anger and grief. A few days later, as the disaster saturates the conscience of the nation, she sends the Duke of Edinburgh to attend the funerals of the children. When he returns and tries to tell her what it was like, he breaks down and his sobs drown out his attempts to describe it. His uncharacteristic emotion pierces the shroud of protocol. Thereafter it's a question not of whether the Queen should go, but when. Eventually, eight days after the tragedy, she goes herself, shares the sufferings of the people, shakes hands, walks through the rubble, and feels in her soul the reality of what had taken place there. Later, we're told, when her private secretary was asked whether the Queen had any regrets over her reign, she replied, 'Aberfan.'

We could very easily say, 'God doesn't do agony, hurt or helplessness: God does creation, colour, life, joy.' But it's not true. We rail at God for suffering and injustice, but God has a one-word answer: Christmas. Christmas isn't a schmaltzy gorging on tinsel, Slade and Amazon. It's a recognition of the brutal reality of human grief and pain. It's a thankful remembrance that God didn't say, 'The deity doesn't do real life.' Neither did God simply send a representative. Instead, God said, 'I'm coming myself.' Christmas means God shows up. Shows up where children lose their parents in war. Shows up where parents lose their children in disaster. Shows up where you face the fear of diagnosis, the agony of relationship break-up, the humiliation of the food bank. Shows up where plans are destroyed, futures stolen, trust betrayed. And Good Friday means that God faces the full consequences of showing up. That's the wonder at the heart of the Christian faith.

And we respond to that wonder with gratitude and a renewed sense of purpose. That sense of purpose can be encompassed in one simple question. 'Where should I show up?' We look at the suffering, tragedy and pain of our world and ask, 'Where should I be showing up? However useless I feel, however little I can do to make a real difference. At whose side do I truly belong?'

My guess is, if you look deep in your heart, you already know the answer. And if you want to know where you're most likely to find Jesus today, that's where. Happy Christmas.

O Little Town of Mariupol

Your classic nativity scene has Mary and Joseph, a baby in a manger, animals choreographed in an arc around them. There may be shepherds, including a child with a lamb, and the odd wise man bearing expertly encased gifts.

The photograph I'm looking at as I write this is a different kind of nativity scene.[1] It depicts Mariupol, on the Sea of Azov at the south-eastern corner of Ukraine, in March. The scene is a war zone, with twisted metal, displaced concrete buildings and

1 Kaamil Ahmed, 2022, 'Ukraine woman who escaped Mariupol maternity ward gives birth', *Guardian*, 11 March, https://www.the guardian.com/world/2022/mar/11/ukraine-woman-who-escaped-mariupol-maternity-ward-gives-birth, accessed 12.04.2023.

the wreckage of apartments. A bloodied woman in bedclothes is picking her way down the stairs. Behind her men in paramilitary gear carry heavy-looking bags. The woman looks dazed. Your eye is drawn to her belly, in the foreground of the picture: she is heavily pregnant.

And it becomes clear what we're witnessing. A woman on the verge of giving birth being led to a safer place. A nativity scene. No ox and ass – instead, recently called-up soldiers. No Joseph – instead, rough but kind strangers, in an act of compassion and solidarity. No manger – but a shattered building.

The woman's name is Mariana Vishegirskaya; she named her baby Veronika, after the woman on the way of the cross who wiped Jesus' bloodied face.

We want Christmas to be cosy, heart-warming, warm and nostalgic. But the first Christmas wasn't. The Jews were under brutal foreign occupation – much as those in eastern Ukraine are today. Mary had to travel while heavily pregnant, on an uncomfortable donkey's back. Soon after the birth, the holy family were forced to migrate to Egypt, a journey scarcely cosier than that which Ms Vishegirskaya in the picture is about to make across Mariupol. Mary's baby was in mortal danger the moment he was born; so was baby Veronika. Mary gave birth with little protection from the elements; Ms Vishegirskaya, about to go out into the snow, had none.

We want Christmas to be so much happier than this Christmas will be. But here's the mystery: Ms Vishegirskaya's experience is closer to the original Christmas than the Christmas we long for. We may be angry, exasperated, humiliated and sad that we can't have the Christmas we want this year. But we're closer, perhaps closer than ever, to the real thing.[2]

---

2 An earlier version of this reflection appeared as Sam Wells, 2022, 'War baby reminds us of what Christmas really means', *London Evening Standard*, 22 December, https://www.standard.co.uk/comment/war-ba-by-christmas-meaning-mariupol-b1048963.html, accessed 12.04.2023.

2

The Word Was Made Flesh: Reflections on Christmas

A present for everybody

I was 12 years old. It was 9pm on Christmas Eve. I had one sister. I realized with horror that I had nothing to give her in the morning. This was the seventies. There were no shops still open. Disaster. My mind traversed the options. Raid my personal library to find a book that looked untouched. Draw a picture of something I could pretend the shop had promised it would have in stock by the weekend. Beg my mother to pass one of her presents off as mine. Needless to say, I pursued the third option. It's still part of my recurring Christmas nightmare. Christmas morning comes and I've forgotten to get the most important person in my life a present.

Of course, if it happened today it wouldn't be a problem. I'd simply slip a note inside a sealed envelope and say, 'In place of a gift a donation has been made of two oxen in the Congo.' Nonetheless it's hard at Christmas to hold the domestic, professional, personal and spiritual dimensions of life together. There's no such thing as a set of Christmas tree lights that work successfully from one year to the next. There's no such thing as a Christmas shopping expedition that goes according to plan. There's no such thing as a male family member over the age of 20 who's easy to buy presents for. There's no such thing as a mother-in-law and daughter-in-law who look forward to cooking turkey together. There's no such thing as a December that goes by without you thinking at some point, 'Why are we doing all this?'

Why *are* we doing all this? We know it's supposed to be about the birth of Jesus, but somehow the biggest gnawing sense of guilt and anxiety is that there won't be a present for everybody. So much of the energy of Christmas comes from the same nightmare I had about my sister. And that's why the drive to make sure every child in our city has at least one present to open on Christmas morning pulls so tight on our heart strings. Because a gift means love, means thoughtfulness, means celebration, and we can't bear to think that there are children in our town or city who have nothing to celebrate, no one to think of them, no experience of love.

But the trouble with giving presents is that what works for one is an insult to another. One person doesn't want a fuss and says just give the money to the food bank; the next person is longing for some gesture of love from you and is deeply hurt and thinks, 'Giving to the food bank is your way of avoiding giving a personal gift to me.' We're all different, and Christmas becomes a test of our love and attention to one another because the inappropriate or thoughtless gift is a sure way of telling our friend or family member that we don't really know them, don't truly care about them, don't deeply understand them.

Just as we're different in our tastes in presents, so we're different in our tastes in faith. We're all true believers about some things and profound sceptics about other things. One person is full of feelings of piety and devotion and yet suspicious of religion being involved in politics and economics. Another person loves the social justice stuff but can never really get their head round the philosophical claims of Christianity. A third finds the beauty of holiness inspiring on an aesthetic level but has never found it straightforward to translate that into trust and faithfulness on the level of relationships. We're all different, and when we meet a Christian whose faith clashes with our scepticism and whose scepticism clashes with our faith, it can be a troubling and confusing experience.

The Christmas story is written for people like us – like all of us, not just people like me or people like you, but for all of us, every different kind of person with every different kind of faith and every kind of scepticism. Let's look at how the story meets each of us right where we are.

Let's say you're sceptical about the divine parts of the story because you believe it's money and politics and global power structures that make the world go round. Well, here's a political story for you. Emperor Augustus is the first person mentioned in the Christmas story. He was known as the prince of peace and the saviour of the whole world, because he'd brought to an end the 15 years of constant war that had beset the Roman Empire since the assassination of Julius Caesar. Luke's story begins with this mighty emperor ruling over the whole world in imitation of God and making a decree that everyone should be registered. This is a political reckoning, because it's a record of how many people he controls and how much money he can squeeze out of them. But it's also an anticipation of judgement, when all the peoples of the earth will be reckoned at the throne of God. Everything in this dimension of the story is saying Jesus is coming into a world of money and international politics. Matthew's story begins with the magi unsettling the local political equilibrium. The magi say there's a new king being born. That sends the local puppet king Herod and the chief priests and scribes into a flurry of anxiety and panics them into murderous reaction. The kind of political realities that brought about Jesus' death are already there at his birth. This is a very political story. If someone says to you, 'Christianity's got nothing to do with politics,' ask them, 'Have you read the Christmas story lately?'

Let's say you're sceptical for a different reason. Let's say for you the realities of life are about relationships and love and kindness and mercy, and Christianity seems to be so mixed up with inhuman institutions and meaningless rituals and abstract doctrines. Well, here's a very human story for you. Mary's expecting a baby. She wasn't planning on it, expecting it, or hoping for it. A pregnancy at 14 years old is no joke. From Mary's point of view, she's aware that this baby is something beyond any conventional imagination. It's hard for her to explain the wonder, let alone the biology, to anyone, maybe most of all Joseph. And think about Joseph. It's bad enough when your fiancée's pregnant and the baby's not yours. Just imagine when all your jealousy and mistrust is directed at the Holy Spirit. I remember a man telling me once how his wife had suddenly become a Christian and how he felt so jealous of the Holy Spirit that she kept talking about the whole time, and how he later came to identify with Joseph whose fiancée seemed physically and spiritually to belong to someone else. And on the most human level it's a confusing and lonely thing to find yourself having your first baby when there's no relatives anywhere around. It's the most physical, emotional and practically demanding experience of your life and in the midst of it you're isolated and alone. And full of fear. Things can go badly wrong in childbirth. The first time Bethlehem is mentioned in the Bible it's a place of personal tragedy. Jacob's wife Rachel, the one he deeply loves, dies giving birth to her second son Benjamin and she's buried at Bethlehem. So this is a very personal and tender story about love and isolation and childbirth and tragedy, and the testing of relationships. If someone says to you, 'Christianity's got nothing to do with my personal experience', ask them, 'Have you read the Christmas story lately?'

Let's say you're sceptical for another reason. Maybe to you, on a scientific level, the whole story seems like a fairy tale. These are not things that happen in everyday life. Well, of course they're not, otherwise we wouldn't be celebrating them as the most precious things in the history of the world. But let's look at what's so miraculous and strange. There's a star that guides the wise men across the desert. That star is telling us that this is a big event in heaven as well as on earth. There's a company of angels who fill the sky and tell the shepherds that the saviour is born. Those angels are messengers – that's what the word angel means – and they mirror on a grand level what the shepherds are called to be on a humble level: messengers of good news to all people, including the despised and outcast shepherds. And there's a virgin birth. That's a way of saying that this is God creating something out of nothing, the same as on the day of creation. It's that significant. So these aren't random fairyland stories. They're communicating the mystery of God's incarnation in the cosmic language of the time. If someone says to you, 'Christianity's got nothing to do with cosmic reality', ask them, 'Have you read the Christmas story lately?'

Let's say you're sceptical for yet another reason. Maybe for you, life in general, and Christianity in particular, is all about compassion and justice and struggling to even the gap between the poor and the rich. It's about empowering those who live with inadequate food, unequal treatment under the law, wretched accommodation, terrible working conditions, or a hundred other burdens in life. And maybe it seems the Christmas story is a sentimental children's tale of little donkeys and dusty roads. Well, look again at the shepherds. These are people excluded from religious society because they can't keep the purity laws due to the nature of their work. Look at the holy family's struggle to find adequate accommodation in Bethlehem. Look at the way Jesus becomes a refugee, his parents departing with him for Egypt when he was just a tiny baby because of their fear of Herod's jealousy. This story has homelessness, economic oppression and forced emigration in it before you've even begun on the tax system and the movement of populations brought about by the census. This is a very contemporary story about social dislocation. If someone says to you, 'Christianity's got nothing to do with social issues', ask them, 'Have you read the Christmas story lately?'

Let's finally say you're sceptical because you can see the social and political and personal humanity in this story, but you just can't make the leap to see it as a story about life, the universe and everything. Maybe for you Christmas is a time for love and family and close relationships and a bit of compassion and generosity, but in general a time for immersing yourself in the good things of the present moment and setting aside life's bigger questions of the origin and destiny of humankind and the universe. Well, Christmas *is* about a beautiful story and all the personal and social and political dimensions we've explored together, but fundamentally the significance of that story is that it tells us the truth about God. And that truth involves two huge philosophical claims. Number one: there is a logic about the way the universe is made, a logic that was there from the very beginning. Number two: that logic, which the evangelist St John calls 'the Word', is not abstract and arbitrary but willed to become human flesh and blood and dwell among us. There's no faraway truth about the universe that's not wholly invested in our present-day reality, and there's no aspect of our present-day reality that's not connected to the ultimate truth about the universe. That's an enormous set of philosophical claims, and the word that Christians use for those philosophical claims is 'Christmas'. So Christmas really *is* about life, the universe and everything. There's no aspect of human life and no dimension of God that isn't wrapped up in Christmas. If someone says to you, 'Christianity's got nothing to do with ultimate truth', ask them, 'Have you read the Christmas story lately?'

Have I missed anybody out? Have I missed out your personal point of faith, or your particular place of scepticism? If I have, I hope I've given you the confidence to rummage around in this awesome story and find the source of your deepest longings and the subject of your deepest questions.

Because what the Christmas story is fundamentally about is God's longing to be present to us in all our political, personal, cosmic, social and philosophical dimensions. There's no part of us that God doesn't want to meet, and no part of the Trinity that God doesn't want to show us in all its glory and wonder and mystery. God really has thought of everything and everybody. And yet God gives each one of us just the perfect present. Anyone would think the Trinity had spent eternity thinking about what would make the perfect present for each one of us. Christmas is the moment when God meets us with the present that has been prepared for every one of us since the foundation of the world. And that present is God: in the least threatening, most needy, least imposing, most irresistible form imaginable: a tiny, helpless baby.

Christmas is really for the grown-ups

Many years ago, I had the opportunity to be in northern India in December. The churches in Delhi had a remarkable tradition I'd never contemplated before. They had nativity plays like everyone else. But all the adult characters – Mary, Joseph, the shepherds, the angels, the wise men, Herod and so on, were played by grown-ups.

I was flabbergasted. How could the church in India have got it so wrong? Surely they must understand that the whole point of nativity plays is that they should be performed by children. Surely December is to be filled by fathers comforting their daughters with the reassuring words that not everyone can play Mary (and that Third Angel really is the crucial role), mothers finding squares of burlap that look convincing on the head of Joseph without being too scratchy, and Sunday School teachers persuading a reluctant wise man from the east that there's a subtle but significant difference between frankincense and Frankenstein. Everyone knows the unique charm of Christmas is lost if adults take it too seriously. I sat there in Delhi and thought, 'Don't these people realize that Christmas is really for the children?'

But look what happens when you see a nativity play performed by adults in a country like India, a place where to be a Christian is always to experience being in a minority, often to face cultural discrimination, and sometimes to find yourself in a place of physical danger. You start to see aspects of the story that get overlooked when it's all about a little donkey on a dusty road.

You see for a start that Christmas is about suffering people. The children of Israel are living in occupied territory. Rome is an empire that has no interest in its subject peoples other than extracting from them money and raw materials. At every place in the Christmas story we see the reality of oppression. The story starts with a census. Why a census? In order to extract more money. Joseph has to travel with his pregnant wife the 100 miles from Nazareth to Bethlehem. Do the authorities care about Mary's condition? Do they compensate Joseph for hours lost at the carpenter's lathe or expenses incurred on an arduous journey? Of course they don't. And then there's Herod, a puppet king suspended by the fragile threads of his own ego. Herod hears of a new king born in Bethlehem and suddenly the knives are out and every boy-child is put to the sword. The holy family emigrate to Egypt, fast as a donkey can take them.

Just look how this story touches on a wide swathe of human suffering. This is a people living in fear, like Iraq under Saddam Hussein or Burma under military rule or the Congo under Mobutu or Ethiopia under Mengistu. Democracy is out of the question, military revolt is absurd, and finding a safe place to survive and thrive is pretty unusual. As often happens with military oppression, we then get displaced populations. Joseph and Mary are first forcibly relocated, like a bunch of people are experiencing right now in Sudan after the independence of South Sudan, or like so many Greeks and Turks were after the creation of modern Turkey in 1922. Then Mary and her husband and baby son find themselves homeless, with no place to stay in Bethlehem. (I wonder whether, while they were homeless in Bethlehem, Joseph saw strangers pointing at him and his family and overheard anyone saying that if he wasn't so lazy and got himself a proper job he wouldn't be homeless. Of course Joseph does have a proper job: he's just been forced out of it by the regime. But maybe the local Bethlehem population isn't all that interested in another sob story.) Then the holy family are forced to become refugees, having to flee Bethlehem for Egypt in search of political asylum.

So this is a story about political oppression, harsh taxes, displaced people, homelessness, unemployment, vulnerable refugees and asylum-seekers. That's the danger of performing it in a place like Delhi and having it acted out by adults who themselves know the very real possibility of any or all of these realities. We might have to recognize what it's really about. And the truth is, we don't want to think about such realities. We don't want to think that our own political system and the demands of our own economy could have comparable effects on far-flung places to those brought about by the Roman Empire and its client regimes all those years ago. We don't want the cosy

Christmas story besmirched by such tawdry human and political realities. We don't want to spoil things by thinking of the oppressed – and more than that, we absolutely can't face the possibility that we might be counted among the oppressors. So we get youngsters to perform our nativity plays. We talk about how magical this season is. We say, 'Christmas is really for the children.' How ... convenient.

But that's not all you find, when you sit in a market square in Delhi and see adults performing the Christmas story in an open-air nativity play. There's more. You see that Christmas is about people struggling, not just politically but personally. Everywhere you look in the Christmas story you see people clinging on with their fingertips to life, to sanity, to respectability, to hope. Luke's gospel starts with Zechariah, serving in the holy of holies in the Jerusalem Temple. It's his big day and all the other priests are waiting for him to come out, and when he does come out he can't say a word. He's the guy who's been waiting all his life for this moment in the limelight, and when it comes he fluffs his lines. Then there's Elizabeth, who's waited all her life to have a baby and it's never come. Adulthood for her has been overshadowed by the monthly disappointments and the social stigma of childlessness. She's got no career to throw herself into: she's simply defined by what she's not. Being defined by what you're not is the essence of poverty.

Then there's Mary. She's got a different personal crisis. She's pregnant and she's clinging to a far-fetched story of who the father is. If you believe that one, you'll believe anything. It's hard enough finding yourself with an unexpected and unwelcome pregnancy in our own culture. Imagine the shame and fear for Mary, in a time when stoning for adultery was not unknown. As for Joseph, consider his humiliation. He's betrothed to this young woman, full of grace, and he thinks he's the luckiest man alive; and then he's made to feel a complete fool – and a heartbroken one at that.

Think for a moment about how large a role shame plays in our culture and in your own life. Shame is crushing, horrifying, terrifying. We'll do almost anything to avoid the searchlight of humiliation. Zechariah, Elizabeth, Mary and Joseph are all in different ways facing up to the reality of shame. At the same time, they're dealing with professional failure, personal disappointment, genuine fear and heart-breaking hurt. Maybe you're in one or more of those places right now. If so, you're in good company.

And even the minor characters in the story are out of their depth. Consider the innkeeper in Bethlehem, trying to accommodate all those extra visitors. He knows what it means to be overwhelmed at work. Consider the soldiers whom Herod sent out to slaughter the innocents. They know what it means to be in a crisis of conscience and to have no respect but plenty of fear for the orders of their boss. Consider the chief priests and scribes that Herod calls in to explain this rumour of the birth of the messiah. They're torn between their longing for the redemption of Israel and their social and economic loyalty to a corrupt regime. Everyone in the story is at a personal crossroads.

The danger of getting adults to perform the nativity story in a fragile emotional environment like downtown Delhi, drenched with beggars, smells, noise and smog, is that Christmas brings us face to face with the personal crises of our lives. The Christmas story's teeming with personal grief, unresolved longings, uncomfortable secrets, shabby compromises, intense fears, social humiliation and aching hurts. We don't want to be reminded of these things at Christmas. The whole point of the holidays is to get together with people with whom you can ignore such things for a few days, and if not be merry, at least eat and drink and enjoy one another for a while. We don't want to think about our own grief and shame, and we certainly don't want to dwell on ways in which our insensitivity or selfishness might be making other's hurts and pain more intense than they already are. So ... we get youngsters to perform our nativity plays. We talk about how magical this season is. We say, 'Christmas is really for the children.' How convenient. How ... safe.

But that's still not all. When you see adults performing a nativity play, not for their grandparents' camera-shots but in order genuinely to inhabit the story and make it their own, you see people not just suffering, not just struggling, but also searching. Look at the wise men. They were scouring the heavens for truth, for meaning, for wisdom, for hope. They took the best science of their day and the courage of their travelling companions and followed the star. Look at the shepherds. They were isolated, cold and frightened, out on the hillside where they couldn't keep the ritual food laws and the only action was a dangerous animal appearing with a taste for woolly sheep or maybe a taste for burlapped shepherd. But they were looking to the heavens too, for hope, for peace, for redemption, for glory. Look at Simeon and Anna in the Temple for baby Jesus' presentation after 40 days. They'd spent their whole lives watching and waiting for the consolation of Israel.

Most of all, think of St John the Evangelist writing his gospel, explaining how this tiny baby was the Word that was from the beginning, was tonight made flesh; and how we have beheld his glory, full of grace and truth. John's searching because he's telling us who Jesus is, what it means that the logic of the universe is encapsulated in this tiny child; but he's also pondering why the saviour was rejected by his own people, why the messiah's coming didn't signal the end of the world, and how evil can abide in the face of such overwhelming goodness.

These are profound searchings, deep ponderings, echoing yearnings. They encourage us to name and explore the edges of our own faith and commitments and convictions and questions. But we don't want to do that at Christmas. The nativity story's full of people searching, people yearning, people wanting to believe that there's more than just appearances and surviving and making a living and staying cheerful. But we don't want those grown-up things. The whole point is to keep it simple: eat, exchange gifts and see loved ones. Maybe watch some TV or get some fresh air. We don't want to think about the great purpose of God in creating and redeeming us, in being with us in Jesus and calling us to be with Jesus in hunger and sickness and imprisonment and on the cross. And we certainly don't want to listen to the searchings of other peoples, faiths or cultures. So ... we find a way to keep things unchallenging and sentimental. We get youngsters to perform our nativity plays. We talk about how magical this season is. We say, 'Christmas is really for the children.' How convenient. How much less demanding than having to think about it all.

Don't get me wrong – I think there's plenty of good reasons to get children to perform nativity pageants. Really. It's good for them to learn the story. It's great for them literally to walk a few steps in the clothes of a shepherd or a teenage mother. It's terrific for grown-ups to gaze on the innocence of childhood and, in so doing, rediscover the wonder of the star, the angels and the baby. Best of all, it may get the adults in touch with the ways the apparently innocent children may not be simply inno-cent at all but in fact be suffering, struggling and searching too, and in the process making the Christmas story their very own.

But be careful. Think again about that nativity play in Delhi. Reflect on the way those grown-ups were in touch with the suffering in this story, the discrimination in their own culture, the political oppression in their own lives. Think about the way those grown-ups were in touch with the struggling in this story, the disappointment, distress and despair in their own lives, and the lives of those around them. Think about the way those grown-ups were in touch with the searching in this story, the unresolved questions of faith, the yearning of people aching for truth, longing for meaning, waiting for hope, reaching out for God. After all, that's what it means to be a grown-up – to suffer, to struggle and to search. And then go back and recog-nize how convenient it is that we make this story for and about children. Because deep down we don't want to see the suffering, we don't want to face the struggling, we don't want to name the searching. We don't really want to be grown-ups.

In the end the good news of Christmas is just this. God, made fully known in Jesus Christ, is with us, in all our suffering, struggling and searching. Beloved friends, Christmas isn't really for the children. It's for you.

Xmas

I want to tell you two stories. They're both stories you may well know. But you may not have heard them told quite like this before.

The first goes like this. Once upon a time all of space was contained in a tiny point. One moment, about 13.8 billion years ago, it exploded, and it's been continuing to expand ever since. After a while, the universe cooled down enough to resolve into atoms. Huge clouds of these elements eventually came together through gravity and formed stars and galaxies. Around 8 billion years later, or two-thirds of the way into the universe's history to this point, the earth was formed by a similar system of gravitational convergence of atoms. A billion years after that forms of life appeared, and about 2 billion years ago oxygen started to be generated by primitive plants. Human beings emerged around 200,000 years ago, which, when you've got used to measuring years in billions, is more or less yesterday.

An unusual, perhaps unique, set of biological and climactic conditions came about to make the beauty and fertility of the world as we know it. The species exist together in remarkable balance and the seasons come and go, replenishing life in the grand sweep of a David Attenborough multi-programme canvas. Patterns of migration and cycles of life lend rhythm and order to what would otherwise seem unfathomable sequences of development and change. After nearly 14 billion years of expansion, and more than 4 billion years of earth, it may seem exaggerated to talk of any threat to this glorious planet and dazzling world. But there are three threats. On a micro level one species, human beings, are setting about dismantling the climactic and biological conditions for the flourishing of all life. On a larger level, some cosmic occurrence like a meteor could always crash into the earth and do untold, perhaps wholesale, damage. And on a macro level just as what comes up must come down, so what expands must, eventually, contract. The largest threat to the earth comes from what many imagine to be a big crunch that will one day, who knows how many billion years away, gravitationally suck the whole shebang back into the tiny mass it was before – then maybe, who knows, to be followed by another Big Bang.

That's the first story. The second story is the same, but very different. You're sitting in a church on Christmas Eve. You've just had a huge row with a member of your family. You wanted the plans for Christmas Day to be a big surprise but the delivery didn't come on time so you had to go to the shops to get something not as good. You're worried that no one will like what you've got for them anyway and part of you is resentful because you know you've put more effort into getting gifts than anyone you're giving them to. You want to sit in church and be happy and festive but your mind is buzzing with a thousand things that don't feel happy and don't feel festive. Your work is going badly and your colleagues are cross and mean, your home needs lots of money spending on it that you haven't got, you've just received a bitter and hurtful email from a person you used to live next door to. The whole idea was that Christmas was supposed to be this oasis of joy in the middle of family, work and neighbourly meltdown. But it isn't working out that way.

Meanwhile a colleague at work has asked to take the day off. She's not done so before, so you ask her why. She says she's picking her family up from the airport. It turns out she managed to escape from a desperate situation in the country she came from and she's spent the last two years living on next to nothing while sending home all her money to her relatives to enable them to escape the way she did. Finally, they've got enough money and they're arriving tomorrow and she's currently got no idea where they're all going to sleep tomorrow night. When you look at the combination of strain, suffering, tiredness, pride and relief on her face you see a whole world of displaced people and cruel regimes and selfless generosity and human ingenuity and you reflect on your own life and wonder if you could ever have achieved what she's achieved.

That's the second story. The first story is epic in scale. It's about billions of years, about indescribable distances and details and dimensions and discoveries. It leaves you thinking, in the context of this massive story, what am I? I'm scarcely a tiny speck in time and space. My existence seems the most colossal chance and my significance seems the tiniest obscurity. The second story is the opposite of the first one. It's ferocious in its intensity. You're totally immersed in the passions and dramas of your life, your fallings-out with one person and tetchy emails to another, your anxiety about one relationship and yearning to enrich a different one, your urgency to get a project finished and your fear about a development that's beyond your control. And the only thing that makes you pause is another person, like you, but not like you, whose story is dominated by political realities you're largely protected from, whose gentle demeanour hides her experience of violence and terror and exploitation and pain, whose every waking moment is designed to free others from the prison she's escaped from, who's absorbed in her world as you are in yours, but whose challenges are on a scale that leaves you humbled.

I said earlier that both stories are the same story. How can this be? The answer is, they're both the Christmas story. The Christmas story is about two words that come together like never before. The first word is 'word' – in Greek '*logos*' from which we get words like biology, anthropology and theology. It means logic. It means the kind of logic of the big bang and all that cosmological language about galaxies and planets. The second word is 'flesh'. Flesh literally means what lives between skin and bone, but in truth it means what I just described in that second story – the human reality of passion and struggle and intensity and hope and despair and grief and love. Flesh means being so angry you can't see straight, being so in love you can't think straight, being in so much pain you can't feel anything else. Logos or word and flesh seem like polar opposites. They both describe our story, what it means to be human both as a result of all those cosmic goings-on and in the midst of strong passions and intense experiences. But what never happens is any overlap, any connection, any intersection between these two stories.

Except once. At one moment in eternity there was a point where word and flesh met. There was an instant in time when the cosmic story and the fleshly story became the same story. That was the moment we call Christmas. The God of heaven and eternity, the God of logic and divine plans, the God beyond and above and forever – took up residence in the world of passion and immediacy and suffering and anger and hatred and love. The word became flesh. This is the story the gospels tell. The heavens moved – the stars were rearranged, the cosmic order stood to attention, the angels lined up to order. The sleepy shepherds and the smelly stable and the earthy manger made a welcome for the bloody, messy, tiny new-born baby. The word became flesh. The cosmic and the earthly intersected. The logic of the stars and the life of the flesh kissed one another. And the result we call Jesus.

When people don't believe in God, it tends to be either because this life, the flesh, is so absorbing in its demands or disappointments or destruction that they can't see anything past it; or because the cosmic realities seem so far away that they can't see any meaning or purpose in any of it. In their own way, these objections make plenty of sense. But neither of these objections reject the Christian God. Because the Christian God brings heaven to earth in being made human, and brings earth to heaven in elevating fleshly life to eternal significance. The whole Christian faith hangs on this moment, when heaven and earth, word and flesh intersect and the two parallel stories become one. The point of intersection we call Jesus. Without Jesus neither story makes any sense. With Jesus we see that they were the same story, waiting to be united at Christmas.

It's quite common as an abbreviation for Christmas to write Xmas. The X is an anglicized version of the Greek letter *chi*, which is pronounced like an English 'k', or 'ch' as in the word charisma. It's the first letter of the word Christ, and so Xmas becomes shorthand for Christmas. But the word Xmas contains a deeper truth. Christmas is the moment of intersection between the cosmos and the intensity of human existence; the coming-together of heaven and earth; the moment the word becomes flesh, and the flesh becomes word. Christmas is the intersection, the moment when the two great stories meet.

Christmas is the crossover, the true X moment. Maybe it should always be called Xmas.

All I want for Christmas is you

When does Christmas happen? Let me explain the question. Christmas starts happening in early October. Shops start tinselling, office parties start booking, people start saying 'We're going to my parents this year as we went to his last year.' But none of those things are Christmas. December's when there are carol services and mince pies and a resolution to make more of an effort to send cards this year and efforts to rescue crushed old tree decorations and lights where one goes out and they all go out. But December isn't Christmas. So when does Christmas happen? I'm going to suggest four different possible answers to that question.

Maybe Christmas happens when you hold a gift on your lap and you genuinely don't know what's inside but you expect you're going to like it. There's a bunch of traditions about what you do next. There's the cherish-in-your-fingers-and-try-to-guess school: only for the very patient and those unworried about keeping everyone waiting. There's the open-carefully-and-save-the-precious-wrapping-paper school: only for the exceptionally tidy and frugal. And there's the tear-open-in-a-frenzy-of-eager-hope school: which only really works if the present really is beyond expectation – otherwise the drooping shoulders and attempt to feign gratitude vividly disclose their own story. But surely that's too worldly to be the heart of Christmas?

Let's try another one. Maybe Christmas happens when the oven door opens and a golden-topped turkey emerges, full of crackling fat, laden with stuffing and bestridden by devils on horseback, followed by pulled crackers, sparklers, absurd puns and respectful silence as the monarch speaks live to the nation of the year's struggles and consolations. That's certainly domestic existence as the adverts portray it, and the scene that almost every celebration in a night shelter or children's home is seeking to replicate. But what exactly do turkeys, crackers, fir trees and dozing grandparents have to do with a baby born in a stable in Bethlehem? Family, food and fun are marvellous things, on their day, but is that really the essence of Christmas?

Let's try a third one. Perhaps Christmas is centrally about worship. After all, angels from the realms of glory came to tell tidings of comfort and joy, shepherds with their flocks abiding left to visit the infant king, three kings came from Persian lands afar. For all we know the ox and the ass and the sheep knelt down and got in on the act; and Mary and Joseph, once the post-natal health and safety check was completed and filed, did their share of adoring too. So maybe gathering in a congregation, doing our best imitation at least of the shepherds, if not the angels and kings; maybe this is when Christmas happens. That's of course what you'd expect a vicar to say. But isn't that missing something a little bit more intimate, a touch more personal? When you leave church at the end of a service, won't you still be thinking that Christmas lies somehow ahead of you – that being together in church is a necessary but not sufficient part of Christmas?

So what is that more intimate, personal touch? Maybe this is getting closer to the heart of it. Christmas is said to be about not receiving, but giving. Perhaps Christmas really happens when you're on a bus, or in a glittering shop, or perhaps today on a website, and you're thinking of a person you care about, and you realize you've identified just the thing that will bring a smile and make them feel understood and listened to and appreciated and loved. After all, what causes the most hurt at Christmas? It's not that Aunty Penny helped herself to all the Quality Street, because she does that every year. It's not that the children got over-excited and there were tears, because no one can have a three-month emotional build-up to some great event without some features causing envy or greed or disappointment. It's that this person, whom you thought knew you, whom you hoped loved you, or at least paid some sort of attention to you, has been totally clueless to get you earrings when it's perfectly obvious your ears aren't pierced, or buy you a tie when everyone knows you never wear one, or not even deigned to set foot in a shop on your behalf or think about you more than five minutes before the exchange of gifts and so just stuffed £10 in an envelope – and to add insult to injury didn't even bother to get a new envelope. If Christmas really is all about the ideal of perfect presents, then we might as well resign ourselves to an annual wake of perpetual failure and festering resentment.

For all these reasons, we're reluctant to commit ourselves to when Christmas happens. We sweep the hand and say, 'It's all of it.' But if it's all of it, does that mean also the awkward parts: the colleague at work you feel you should be kind to but just thinking about it brings to the surface all the anger and irritation of a year of undeclared war; the post-dinner washing up that no one feels in the mood to do; the eagerness to close the door on anything and anyone that might seem cold, or needy, or sad, or alone in an impulse to don the Christmas sweater and be hearty, warm and ready to refill the glass for another drink? Here's the paradox of Christmas. We aren't really sure when Christmas really happens, so to hide our anxiety we tend to crowd the season with celebration, half-finished conversations and rapidly purchased, less-than-suitable presents, as if the festive season were an overfull Christmas stocking packed tightly with trinkets, lest we ever look closely enough at any of them to wonder if they're of any real value.

So when does Christmas happen? I'll tell you when I think Christmas happens. Think about a moment around 8.30 in the evening of Christmas Day. All the flurry is over, wrapping paper's strewn around, the chocolate box is open and half-finished, the coffee cups haven't made it back to the kitchen, it's gone dark outside but no one's yet had the energy to get up and put a light on. A child of about eight years old has found a quiet place in the semi-darkness. On closer inspection the child is holding something. There's been a stocking. There's been money from Aunty Penny who said, 'Go get yourself something in the sales.' There's been some other gifts. But sitting in a corner in the twilight, this child is holding tight to just one present. That one present represents hope fulfilled, perhaps exceeded, joy awaited, imagination engaged, love expressed, needs met, longings understood, excitement ahead. It's already obvious that when bedtime comes that present is going on the bedside table or under the pillow. Right now, it's not clear if this child is ever going to let that present out of its sight till kingdom come. That intensity, that certainty, that fixed attention and unswerving clasp rather puts in the shade the crammed stocking and the litany of gifts. In the end, there was only one present that mattered. This one. In time, the other gifts may or may not get a swift glance; but this one is the precious one. This one is Christmas.

I want you to focus all your energy and wonder on this child right now, and on the present in this child's hands. Who is this child? And what is the significance of that present? The answer to this question is what Christmas is all about. This child is God the Father who made the world as a playground of delight, a place of encounter and relationship and trust restored, and talents expressed and beauty perceived and truth embodied. This child is God the Son who adores us so much that he never lets go, who goes to any lengths to be with us, who bears the cost of our folly in his own body: if you look closely at this child, you'll see he's holding the present with hands that have marks of nails and blood and pain and love. This child is God the Holy Spirit who weaves a pattern of hope around and between us, who reconciles and heals and sings God's song in our hearts, who makes something wondrous even out of the mess in which we leave things. If you get near to that child, you can hear her whispering, humming and singing to the present about how cherished and beloved it is. This child is God.

And what is that present? That present is you. For you God the Father longs and yearns and dreams and hopes. For you God the Son becomes flesh and lives and dies and is raised again. For you God the Holy Spirit plays and weaves and dances and heals. Christmas is the moment in history when we see into the heart of God. And what we see is that God could have anything – God could have any present in the universe, God could have stars or waterfalls or meteors or big bangs or rainbows or galaxies or black holes or comets. But at the end of all things, when all the good and all the failed ideas and wonders of creation are lying littered across the floor of God's living room, what do we see but God, a small child, cherishing, relishing, holding, beholding the one thing that matters: us.

At Christmas, God the Father says, 'I made creation so as to be with you.' At Christmas God the Son says, 'I want to be with you in flesh and blood, in sorrow and in joy, in tragedy and hope.' At Christmas God the Holy Spirit says, 'I will be with you always. Nothing can separate us.'

That's what Christmas is. That's when Christmas happens. When we realize only one thing matters, only one thing lasts forever, only one thing's in God's heart. When in the darkness we hear a little child softly singing and we realize that little child is God, and we recognize the words God's singing: 'All I want for Christmas is you.'

Take it as a compliment

From an early age almost all of us have a craving for attention. A young child will sit at the top of the slide and say, 'Look at me!' insistently before settling for the secondary pleasure of actually descending to the bottom. The real reward is the clap, the laugh, the admiration – in the case of the parent, the reflected glory that says, 'I have produced a child that can go down a slide!' As we grow older, we get more sophisticated in our desire to be noticed and appreciated – but like the little child, our endeavours can often be undertaken as much for the acclaim that may accompany them as for their value in themselves. Yet when and if the reward does come, it invariably arrives in a different form from that which we were anticipating, and we often make a complete hash of receiving the compliment.

Let's imagine you're a man and you've been invited to a Christmas party and thought long and hard about what shirt to wear: not too smart and not too casual, apparently effortless but carefully matching our eyes and shoes. Sure enough, we've not been at the party two minutes before someone says, 'Lovely shirt.' We don't really know what the remark means. It could be a come-on, saying, 'And a lovely body in that shirt.' Or it could be a criticism, meaning, 'The rest of you's pretty awful, but at least the shirt's OK.' It could be a nod to our good taste, implying, 'You clearly know what to look for in the shops.' Or it could be a sly insult to our income level, suggesting, 'Considering the budget you're on, you got an artificial fibre that looks just like silk – I was almost fooled.' Most likely it's an innocent but tender gesture, hinting, 'Seeing you dressed up all classy makes me realize how much I like and appreciate you.' But all these interpretations rush through our head at the same time and as often as not, out comes something disastrous.

We blurt out something like, 'It's the only thing I had in the wardrobe that didn't need ironing.' In the process we clumsily reveal too much about our lazy domestic habits, turn the compliment into a criticism and deflate the whole spirit of the conversation, giving the other person nothing to say. We were trying to be humble but we end up being almost hostile. What we should do is, succinctly and sincerely, look the person in the eye and simply say, 'Thank you.' But we don't. We make it awkward, cross our arms to protect ourselves, look at the floor, maybe blush, or glance awkwardly elsewhere, as if to say we don't trust the motives of the speaker or we've got more interesting things on our mind.

Another way to deflect the compliment is to whack the ball straight back across the net and say, 'I was going to say the same about your shoes, they're amazing' – which is really a way of saying, 'I can't stand the spotlight being on me, or at least not about my shirt. They could at least have noticed my nobility of soul and my deep and profound wisdom, or my other outstanding qualities.' Or we push the compliment aside and say, 'Actually I don't like it very much, but my sister gave it to me and I knew she was going to be here.' This is really saying the other person has bad taste and flawed judgement – and in a subtle way it may be hinting, 'Actually I'm so classy I even look good in something tawdry like this shirt, and like a lot of people you're clearly so mesmerized by me you can't tell the difference between stylish and lame.' Or we can go to the extreme of squeezing out more affirmation, asking, 'What do you like about the shirt? Do you think it goes well with my eyes?' Or, even more egregiously, 'I bought this shirt on the day I got 55 A stars in my A-levels, and it always makes me feel great.'

In all these ways our quest for affirmation and recognition founders on the rocks of our suspicion, clumsiness and crushing self-doubt. We're longing to matter, to have some impact on the world, and if that stunning effect isn't overwhelmingly obvious to ourselves and others and indisputably triumphant and compelling, we settle for acclaim and warm appreciation from a bevy of admirers, or maybe a single kind remark. But somehow, whatever acknowledgement we receive it's never quite enough and we languish in reproach of the watching world for its lack of gratitude and applause, or we spiral in self-rejection for our fraudulent claims to be a decent, interesting, stable, attractive or accomplished human being. Each compliment becomes further evidence of our isolation, further demonstrating that the rest of the world has no idea who we really are, for good or ill.

Eighteen hundred years ago the Roman emperor and philosopher Marcus Aurelius offered a way out of this impasse about compliments. He coined the phrase, 'Imitation is the sincerest form of flattery.' In other words, the best compliment is the unspoken one, when a person adopts your form of dress, behaviour, speech or lifestyle. That's the point when you know a compliment is genuine – when the other person actually has skin in the game and alters their life to be more like yours, even (or especially) if they don't realize they're doing it.

Christmas is just that kind of compliment. God knows human beings are restless, looking for affirmation, full of self-doubt, insecure, and that such anxiety makes them envious, manipulative, suspicious, deceiving and egotistical. Here's the great mystery of Christmas: why, given God's comprehensive understanding of how flawed, fallen, feckless, foolish and feeble we can be, did God want to be in relationship with us at all? There isn't an answer to this question; it's a profound mystery, per-

haps the deepest mystery of them all. But the truth of Christmas
is this: Jesus wanders into the party and pays us the greatest
compliment in the history of existence. He becomes one like us.
He flatters us by imitating us: no, more than flattery, because
it's based on the truth not a lie, and because it's not designed to
seduce us or gain advantage over us; and more than imitation,
because Jesus goes beyond imitating us and fulfils all the potential of being human that we never realized.

Jesus doesn't compliment us by just taking the nice and pre-
sentable parts of our existence. He's conceived at a time his
mother isn't married. He transforms the social status of ritually
unclean underclass shepherds and triggers a vast journey of
generally unwelcome and untrustworthy foreign philosophers
from the east. He narrowly escapes a genocidal attack by the
local mayor. He becomes a refugee. And that's just as a baby.
Later he faces homelessness, hostility, betrayal, denial, aban-
donment, torture and crucifixion. He sees the worst in our
nature and experiences the most agonizing depths of our suffering. There's nothing sentimental or nostalgic about Christmas. It's God entering the most hostile and terrifying realities
of being human.

But Christmas isn't just the greatest imaginable compliment
any of us could ever be paid. It's a redefinition of what it means
to be human. Whatever our walk in life, be it as a soldier who's
seen the savagery of war, a business person who's known how
customers and staff can behave, a teacher who's seen every kind
of pupil, or a cleaner who knows what people leave in their
bins, we may come to believe we've seen what human beings
are really like – and it's ugly. But Christmas, the coming of God
as a baby amongst us, changes our default understanding of
what humanity is. People can be selfish, but Jesus gives up his
life for those yet unborn. People can be cruel, but Jesus answers
hatred with kindness. People can be violent, but Jesus forgives
his killers from the cross. People can be merciless, but after his
resurrection Jesus seeks out Peter and gives him a new job to
do. People can be judgemental, but Jesus says let the one without sin cast the first stone. This is what humanity is and this is

how we were made to be: wholly at peace with ourselves, with one another, with creation and with God.

Don't take God putting on our flesh in Jesus as a fanciful folk tale or a faraway fairy story. Don't take it as a judgement on our mistakes or a condemnation of our whole self. Don't take it as an exposure of our failure or a threat to our identity. *Take it as a compliment.* Take it as the biggest compliment that's ever been paid in the history of existence. Take it as the compliment that defines your life. Take it as a compliment that means you never need another compliment again. Of course it's nice when people say flattering things, when they're generous, thoughtful, perceptive and kind. But when your whole being, down to the tiniest atom, has been utterly validated and raised to its highest possible potential by the one who knows us before we are born and sees the truth in our hearts and has prepared for us life beyond forever, then no compliment can ever come near you again, because you've been shown who you are and who God is, and how the two can never be parted again.

And if you're moved by this wondrous compliment, if you're delighted, transformed, awestruck and overwhelmed by the gift of God in Christ becoming a tiny baby in all that vulnerability and detail and glory, and if you're longing to give God a compliment in return, not just a trivial remark but something genuine and worthy and heartfelt and true, then know that there's only one kind of compliment Jesus wants in return. There's only one kind of compliment that Christmas deserves. There's only one kind of compliment that's free of superficiality or deception or mixed motives or manipulation. And that's imitation.

The compliment God wants is that we imitate Jesus. Live generously the way he lived. Be merciful the way he was. Love the outcast the way he loved. Spend time with the people he spent time with. Imitation is the only flattery God wants.

One day, finally, you will stand before Jesus and see him face to face, having walked in his steps and followed his paths. These are the words he'll say to you: 'You look just like me.' And this is what you'll reply: 'Take it as a compliment.'

The light still shines

During the pandemic in 2021 I discovered a man with a unique story to tell. He'd been left in St Martin-in-the-Fields as a baby. No one ever found his birth mother. He was called Martin, after the patron saint of our church. He was given as his birthday the day he was found in the church. The year was 1938.

He's still alive. He's had an unusual life, a lot of it spent on the Dutch West Indian island of Curaçao, some in Surrey, and a good deal as a TV engineer.

A week later I had a letter enclosing a donation to St Martin's. The woman who wrote it said the donation was in memory of her parents. Her parents, she said, had been greatly helped by St Martin's and had never forgotten the kindness shown to them. The year they were helped was 1938.

It struck me that these two stories are both versions of the Christmas story. In the second, a young couple with nowhere to turn find shelter and warmth – just as Joseph and Mary did in Bethlehem. In the first, a baby comes into the world with a tough yet miraculous beginning – and goes on to live a remarkable life.

Both are stories about how the Christmas story became flesh in 1938. Both are also about how the Christmas story becomes flesh today. In 1938 on the brink of war; and in 2021 in the midst of a pandemic. The light still shines: the darkness has not overcome it.

3

The Image of the Invisible God: Reflections on the Incarnation

Christ the camera

I have a friend who gives the same Christmas present to his wife every year. Round about the beginning of December he gathers together all the photographs he's taken over the previous twelve months and picks out a dozen that he likes the most. He then arranges them in a frame, and writes in the number 2023, or whatever the year is. Finally, he chooses the one picture that sums up the whole year and puts it in the middle and fits a glass on the frame and wraps it up and lays it under the Christmas tree. His dining room is now crowded with a constellation of memories. He somehow uses his camera to order his world, to shape his memories and to identify the heart of things. That camera is the real centre of his life.

The gospel writers do something quite similar when they arrange a host of visual images in a kind of a circle within the frame of the Christmas story. The Christmas story isn't so much the highlights of 0 BC, or 4 BC or 8 BC or whatever year it was – it's more like the highlights of world history. Think for a moment about the photographs that are gathered round the outside of the frame.

Think first of all about creation itself. That's got to be one of the highlights. The God who made the heavens and the earth gives us a little reminder by setting a star in motion to cross the sky and lead the magi to the stable. So we start with a photograph of the star, to show us that God is the God of science and the universe and all the galaxies and black holes and big bangs.

And then there's Herod. Other politicians are mentioned in the Christmas story, including the Emperor Augustus and the Governor Quirinius. But the photograph has to be of Herod, the half-Jewish envious puppet king, furious at news of a pretender to his throne and showing us that this is a story about politics, power, alliances and uneasy heads that wear a crown. In Herod's photograph we see that God has always been involved in politics, but seldom in the way that those who are in charge want him to be.

And then there's the wise men themselves. Here's a third photograph, to show us what religion and philosophy can do. These magi are people who had spent their lives pondering the inner and outer mysteries of the universe, and the summit of their searchings took them across the desert of human ignorance to the very threshold of God's revelation. The picture shows us that other religions and philosophy can take us to Jerusalem, but not quite to Bethlehem. They can take us to the throne, but not to the manger. Close – but not quite there. The picture of the wise men shows us the best that historical human endeavour can achieve.

And of course there's the shepherds. Here are a group of people at the bottom of the social pile. Their kind of work excluded them from the religious rituals of cleansing and eating that separated out the holy from the unwashed. They were dirty, uneducated and generally despised. But the shepherds' photograph in our Christmas frame shows their faces lit up by the angels' light, their hearts lifted high by the amazing news, their tongues singing with the joy now come to the world. This picture shows us that God is closest to those the world keeps at a distance.

And don't forget Joseph. He is a man who dreams. His photograph ought to show him asleep, because four times, like his Genesis namesake with the technicolour dreamcoat, he dreams. He dreams that the child is God's son. He dreams that Herod means trouble and Egypt's the best place to run to. He dreams that it's time to come home. And he dreams that Nazareth has the cheapest real estate these days. And the photograph shows us that God works through the conscious and the subconscious, that the nether world of dreams just as much as the concrete world of reality is the theatre of God's glory.

Next to Joseph has to be the photograph of Mary. Here we see an open mouth when the angel appears, an open mind when the angel talks tall, an open heart to be the handmaid of the Lord, and finally, though hidden for modesty's sake, an open womb in which a new creation can begin to take shape. And Mary's photograph shows us that God isn't just the God of science and politics and philosophy and the supernatural and social justice, but that God is the God of family drama, of unforeseen pregnancy and paternal jealousy and community embarrassment and the mundane and glorious experience of a young woman bringing a child into the world.

And then finally there's the angels. One comes to Zechariah. One comes to Mary. One comes to Elizabeth. First one, then a whole multitude come to the shepherds. Now that's what I call a spectacular photograph. And what do these angel photographs tell us? They show us that God is orchestrating an extraordinary symphony, a unique drama in which all kinds and manners of people, rich and poor, Jew and Gentile, male and female, ruler and oppressed, and indeed the whole created order is constellated around one event, one definitive event.

And the truth is that none of these photographs is the central picture. They're all the pictures that are arranged around the image that says it all. And that central photograph is not a grand mathematical theorem or an as yet unseen intergalactic phenomenon. That central photograph is not of an elected president or a self-aggrandizing tyrant. That central photograph is not of a great philosophical breakthrough or a meeting of the world's religious leaders. That central photograph is not of a march for justice or an act of social protest. That central photograph is not of an inspiring dream, for this country or for the world. That central photograph is not even of a person for once faithful to God's will.

That central photograph is of a baby. A baby wrapped in swaddling clothes and laid in an animal's feeding trough.

Christianity is certainly about all the things portrayed in the other photographs – it's about science, it's about politics, it's about philosophy, it's about justice, it's about dreaming dreams, it's about faithful discipleship and it's about God working in history. But fundamentally Christianity begins here – with a tiny baby.

And that baby changes the way we think about science, because here at the heart of things is vulnerable, fragile, human life and human relationship. All the battles about science and religion seem to miss this tiny baby at the centre of it all. And that baby changes the way we think about politics, because the way God exercises power, when he has all the power in the universe at his disposal, is by coming among us as a defenceless baby. And that baby changes the way we think about philosophy, because at the end of all our ponderings and wonderings there is not an idea but a child, not a word but soft, infant flesh. And that baby changes the way we think about justice because the way God calls for justice is not with a campaign on the streets or a bill in Congress but with a piercing cry and an insatiable need for milk. And that baby changes the way we think about dreams because now all our dreams are focused on what this child has brought us. And that baby changes the way we think about discipleship because now we see that caring for babies, caring for refugee and displaced babies, caring for babies arising from unexpected pregnancies and bringing about social embarrassment, caring for babies amid violence and hatred and hardship and fear is the way we worship the God we find in this central photograph, the God we meet in this baby.

God creeps into the hostile territory of human life under the radar. God comes not with an earthquake or in a spaceship or after a lightning flash or at the end of a bloodthirsty battle. God enters the drama in the most tiny, most ordinary and yet most conventionally miraculous way of all – through an everyday but still breath-taking human birth. Jesus is born in much the same way in which he dies. He is naked. He is laid on wood. His arms are restrained so that he cannot even scratch his face. And there are no more than a couple of friends or relatives there to mark the momentous occasion. This is an awesome drama, but its awe lies not in its wide screen but in the intensity by which the whole history and meaning and purpose of creation are concentrated in this precious moment, this tiny body, these vital relationships, this vulnerable life.

Think with me once again about the camera for a moment. I was never the most conscientious student of physics, but one lesson from my youth has stayed with me all these years. We made a pinhole camera. On one side of the camera was the whole world – of trees and cars and buildings and people. On the other side was a camera film. In between was a piece of cardboard. And in the centre of the cardboard was a tiny, almost invisible hole. And what happened was that somehow all the light from the world outside got transported through that tiny hole and reproduced an image on the camera film a few inches beyond it. But the image was the wrong way up (because light travels in straight lines) so the light from the top of the building ended up at the bottom of the image. I remember my physics teacher saying that pinhole cameras require longer exposure times than other cameras – sometimes several seconds, sometimes several hours. I was such a poor student of physics that in my case maybe 30 years would have been a better estimate.

But here's the mystery of the incarnation – the wonder of Christmas. Christ is the camera. The baby Jesus is that pinhole. All the myriad diversity and extent of the universe, its science, its politics, its philosophy, its struggle for freedom, its dreams, its faithfulness – all of that is concentrated in this tiny baby, this almost invisible fleshly presence. And all the wondrous diversity and extent of God is in this baby too. And this baby, this pinhole in which is concentrated all the light that enlightens the world, does an extraordinary thing. This baby takes the light of the world, takes all the science and the politics and the wonder and the struggle and all the rest, and turns them upside down. This baby turns the world upside down. This baby is the image of the invisible God, as St Paul calls him. This baby is eternity in an instant. This baby overturns every image and reality and certainty the world ever had.

My friend had it just right, having a camera at the centre of his life, and he had it just right each Christmas, gathering a constellation of pictures around one central picture. But God has a slightly different camera and slightly different pictures. Christ is the camera. The tiny, vulnerable baby is the image that takes the wondrous extent of the whole world and turns every tiny piece of it upside down. That's the good news of Christ's incarnation. That's the good news of Christmas.

Oh, and there's one more thing about that camera, about that central image, about that Jesus, about that tiny, swaddled, vulnerable, pinholed baby. It needs a long exposure time. You need to give it a very, very long exposure time. Happy Christmas.

Four mysteries and a truth

Christmas night is a moment of great wonder. It is a night when a new baby is wrapped in swaddling clothes and when our Christian faith is shrouded in mystery. We come, like the shepherds, like the magi, to worship the new-born king, to find in him the truth about the world, the truth about ourselves, the truth about God. But to get to this truth, to experience this truth, we need first to appreciate the mystery, the four-fold mystery of God's heavenly drama. We need to rediscover Christmas, the cosmic thriller of four mysteries and a truth.

The first mystery is this. Why did God bother to create the universe? Think of it. A hundred million stars in every galaxy, a hundred million galaxies in the universe. Why? Why this astonishing, colossal project that defies description or comprehension? And why did God create life on this planet, tucked away in an obscure corner of that vast universe? Why did God bother? Surely there must have been more pressing projects to take on. Surely there must have been a nagging thought, 'Will I regret it?' What an overwhelming universe it is. And here, in a little corner of it, Earth, seas, land, mountains, reptiles, insects, plants, animals – and human beings, you and me. And that is the first mystery: why did God bother?

And the second mystery is like unto it, thus. Why, given the mess we made of things, did God continue to bother? Why did God not give up on us when humans turned out the way they did? The Old Testament is a passionate story of love and hate, delirious joy and crushing disappointment. For reasons that are a mystery, God sent a rainbow to Noah and promised never to destroy the earth again. But why God made that promise and whether it became a matter of regret, who can say? Why did God continue to bother? I expect you're familiar with annual family updates that say how young Freddie is now a neurosurgeon, Daisy has just won the Nobel Prize for astrophysics, but Sally ... Sally, sadly, is still ... well, who knows what next year will bring? Imagine God's annual update. Venus has grown up a lovely girl, Mars is a real sweetie, Mercury has his ups and downs, but Earth ... Earth still seems unable to help herself and struggles with the simplest practices of peace – but, well, who knows what next year will bring? Fancy writing the same letter for thousands of years. That's the second mystery. The first mystery is why does God bother; the second is why does God continue to bother.

The third mystery seems to be the greatest mystery of all. It is the most baffling part of the whole story. Given that God bothered to make the universe and the world within it, given that God continued to bother with the world despite the way things turned out, the unfathomable mystery is this: why do we not bother – why can we not be bothered? I don't know if even God has the answer to this one. It defies all logic. We have been given this whole world, a playground of delight. We have been given time and space to grow and learn and experiment and discover. We have been given taste to relish, sight to dazzle, touch to treasure, hearing to enthral. We have been given beauty beyond value, music of the heavens, hearts to love and minds to ponder. Most of all we have been given a story that makes sense of the whole mystery, an invitation that shows us where we fit in to this great cosmic drama, a promise of companionship with God and a place at his table forever. And yet we can't be bothered. We leave half the Christmas gifts unopened and go and sulk in our bedroom. And if someone asks us what the matter is we are baffled to find an answer. We can't be bothered, can't be bothered to join the dance of God's glory, can't be bothered to enter the garden of his delights, find no reason to explore the palace of his unending peace. What a startling mystery: why do we not bother?

And it is in the context of these three mysteries that we approach the mystery of Christmas. Given that God had bothered to make the universe and place us in it, given that God had continued to bother over it, given that we couldn't be bothered, why on Christmas night, why at backward Bethlehem, why to a child-mother in an obscure cattle-shed – why, when God chose to enter the story, to be bothered so much as to set aside all the trappings of majesty – why did God come with so little bother? Why was Jesus wrapped in humble rags, not robes of gold, why was Jesus laid in a dirty feeding trough, not a jewel-encrusted four-poster bed? Why didn't God trumpet the whole world and make them notice, make them be bothered? Why was there no broadcast to the whole universe that the saviour of the world was coming to town? Why did Jesus come as a baby at all, and not a mighty warrior for justice and truth? Where was the anger, where was the fury, where was the righteous resentment that said 'You have rejected my openhearted love, ignored my bountiful promises, scorned my kingdom of peace? This is the fourth mystery – why did God come with such little bother?

Four mysteries that go together to make up the drama of Christmas. But I promised you that I would not just show you a great mystery, I would show you perhaps an even greater truth. The truth is simply put. God did bother. And, just as significantly, still does. And the key to it lies in one detail that is so important to Luke's story that he repeats it in case we didn't catch it the first time. We are so familiar with the Christmas story – the story of the little donkey, the dusty road, the starry night, the cattle lowing, the series of Bethlehem hotels bursting with travellers, the tired innkeeper, the bed of straw. None of these staple nativity ingredients are in the Bible, of course. So, what is in the Bible – what does Luke regard as crucial to the story of Jesus' birth? 'She wrapped him in swaddling clothes and laid him in a manger.' Luke tells us twice.

Swaddling clothes. Bands of cloth. Very, very ordinary. In fact, so ordinary that it's hard to see why Luke tells us once, let alone twice. Aren't all babies wrapped in bands of cloth after they are born? It's easier to understand the detail about the manger. Jesus was born in very humble circumstances – homeless, almost out of doors, in the cold – and his first worshippers were social outcasts, shepherds, the socially and ritually excluded of their day. That's what the manger tells us. But bands of cloth? What is strange about that? Well, nothing, except it makes a point that Luke comes back to at the end of his gospel. At the two defining moments in Jesus' life, his birth and his death, he is utterly powerless – so powerless that he cannot use his arms. Here at his birth, his arms are strapped to his sides by swaddling clothes – Luke tells us this twice, remember, and the angels tell the shepherds that this will be the 'sign'. And later at Jesus' death his two hands are nailed to either end of a horizontal beam, and as he dies in agony he cannot even wipe his own brow or scratch an itch or waft away a fly or mosquito. These are the most intimate moments in Jesus' life, and at both moments, by swaddling clothes and by nails , he is, literally, disarmed.

This is the astonishing truth of Christmas. Jesus is God disarmed. The disarmed and disarming love of God. And this is the closest God gets to revealing to us the secret of the four great mysteries. The first mystery, you'll remember, is 'why did God bother?' – why did God bother to create the universe. The answer must be, because of this moment, this breathtakingly beautiful moment when earth and heaven were joined in perfect harmony, when there was a new creation, fully human and fully God, the unchanging wonder of God in one flesh with the transient being of humankind. The possibility of friendship, of God and us as true companions, embodied in the life of a single being. Jesus is the reason for the universe and Jesus is the meaning of the universe. This tiny baby, wrapped in swaddling clothes and just alive – he is meaning of life, the universe and everything. That's why God bothered to create the universe – to be our friend in Jesus.

And the second mystery, you'll remember, is 'Why did God continue to bother?' – why, given the way the world turned out, did God not just give it up as a bad job. The answer to this mystery must be that there is a difference between something being happy and something being beautiful. God transformed the horror of our sinfulness into the glory of Christ's incarnation. God made the world to be happy, but when it turned nasty God made it beautiful instead. God continued to bother because glory could be revealed not just in wondrous creation but even more in transforming love. And that newborn child in swaddling clothes shows us both creation and transformation.

Now the final mystery, 'Why did Christ come in this way?', why did God come with so little bother, comes into view. We spend all our Christian life learning and trying to be God's child and here all our efforts are turned upside down, because on this night, born of Mary, God is our child. Not the loving parent but the needy child. Of all the extraordinary ways Mary's prophetic song comes true, this is surely the most vivid. God puts down the mighty from their seat and exalts the humble and meek. God comes down from the mighty seat of being our loving father and becomes our child, and meanwhile exalts us, meek children, and makes us, in Mary, the parent. Did ever a revolution in history compare to this? Can we comprehend what we are seeing? Almighty God become a tiny baby. The one who made the starry height is laid upon our arms tonight. We spend all our Christian life praying to Almighty God, and here is God, face to face with us for the first time, wrapped in swaddling clothes, unable to move a finger. We read constantly in the Old Testament of God's outstretched hand and mighty arm, but here God is, wrapped in bands of cloth – if you'll forgive the pun, armless. Nothing can ever be the same again – childhood, parenthood, faith, reality. Jesus is God disarmed. The disarming love of God.

But, you'll say, you can't stop there – you've missed a mystery out. The third, perhaps the most unfathomable mystery of all.

Why, if God bothered and continued to bother and came to reveal and revolutionize reality yet with so little bother – why, why oh why, can we not be bothered? Why do we so perversely turn away from the limitless wonder and glory of God? Why do we spurn his constant invitation of undying love and constant friendship? I am not going to answer that one for you. You can only answer that for yourself. But once again the swaddling clothes give us the clue to God's response. God in no way forces us to love. God wants our hearts. So Jesus comes to us, tiny, naked, artless, needy and wrapped in bands of cloth, to show there is no catch, no hidden trick, no clever device to ensnare or entrap us. Do we not find the innocence of this love disarming? Is it not time to put down our weapons of defence against God, our pointless war against goodness, truth and beauty, and be disarmed by this swaddled bundle of joy and gladness? God is with us, in a tiny, defenceless baby being held out by a poor, overwhelmed young mother. She is holding him out to you. This is God, for you, disarmed. Take him, hold him, embrace him. How can we refuse him?

And was made man

We're near the start of the movie. The camera pans round a dimly lit control room, with a large screen on one side and row upon row of highly trained consultants staring at sophisticated computers all around them. The men have sleeves rolled up a little and ties loosened, to show they're under pressure and working hard. The women are humourless and magnificently professional. The workstations emit periodic electronic beeps, to show they're at full output and being constantly primed with relevant data. Then, from behind one computer, comes a trembling shout. A tired but incredibly intelligent data analyst clutches a print-out and draws a crowd around a radar screen. With a sudden silence in the control room, and a crowd of analysts clustering around, nervously pointing to the bottom corner of the screen, beads of sweat appearing on his forehead, he says to his overwrought but compassionate boss, 'See, there. That … that thing. We don't know what it is. We've done all the checks, captain, but there's no record of anything like this. It's alive. But it's like nothing this planet has ever seen before.' Cue dramatic music, roll opening credits over scenes of scrambled aircraft, hastily convened presidential press conferences and passionless voices broadcasting calls for calm. It may just be a blob on a radar screen – but you can be sure we'll spend the next 87 minutes finding out whether we can blow it up before it destroys us.

We have bated breath each Christmas night because we believe that Jesus Christ, born around 2,000 years ago this night, is like nothing this planet has ever seen before. We've done all the checks, captain, but there's no record of anything like this. The first question asked of Jesus in the gospel of Mark is, 'Have you come to destroy us?' The story of the gospels is that people treat Jesus like a space alien and try to destroy him before he destroys them. But Jesus isn't a space alien. Jesus is a love letter from God to humankind. Jesus is the place and the person where God meets us and we meet God. Jesus is humanity and God in the most intimate relationship imaginable: one flesh, one person.

After many years studying theology, I've concluded there's one question that's more significant than all the others. It's not 'Does God have a white beard?' It's not 'What would Scooby Doo?' It's not about suffering or other faiths or who gets to heaven or unanswered prayer. This is the question: If there'd been no fall, if humankind had never sinned, would Christ still have come? Is the coming of God in Christ as fully human and fully God, what we call the incarnation – the event we celebrate at Christmas – the beginning of a rescue package that bails humanity out of suffering and sin and death and evil, God's down-payment on a deal that's finally clinched on Good Friday and Easter Day? Or is Christmas even more mysterious still? Why did Jesus come among us? It's a question that takes us into the very heart of God.

The great theologians of the early centuries came up with one succinct answer. They said, 'He became what we are so that we might become what he is.' Jesus became human like us so that we might become divine like him. That's the classic answer to the question. I know a man who owned his own plane and lived beside an airfield. One day he was tuned into his shortwave radio and heard a distress call from a pilot in the skies above who was lost in bad weather and almost out of fuel. He tuned in and asked her what she could see. Quickly he realized where she was and replied, 'I'm coming up to get you.' When he drew near, he said on the intercom, 'Look across – I'm right beside you, I'm not going anywhere, I'll be with you all the way.' Not long later both planes were at the airfield and she was safely drinking cocoa at his house, shaken but glad to be alive.

That's the classic answer. We're the pilot in distress, lost in bad weather and running out of fuel. 'He became what we are so that we might become what he is.' Somehow the whole of Jesus' story, his birth, life, ministry, passion, death, resurrection and ascension, is in that short phrase. 'He became what we are so that we might become what he is.' Note that he didn't become what we are in every respect. He didn't become a sinner. But he became what we are in our human limitations, in being subject to pain and suffering, and death. Like a New York firefighter climbing the stairs of the World Trade Center on 9/11, he came to where we were and, with a great bear hug, embraced us and brought us to where he is, brought us to safety at great cost to his own life, brought us home.

The classic answer shows us that in Jesus we've seen what God and humanity truly look like. Jesus reveals what it means to be human and what it means to be God. In Jesus the wall between humanity and God is replaced by a window. God sees us, and we see God, like never before. And the mystery of Christmas is this: Jesus shows us that at the heart of what it means to be human is to be wrapped up in God; and at the heart of what it means to be God is to be wrapped up in humanity. This is our Christmas present.

So the classic answer to the question of why Jesus came is that he had a job to do: to rescue us from sin and human limitations so that we might come to share the divine life. But for all that the classic answer shows us about who Jesus is, it leaves one important question unanswered. Was the incarnation something that came out of overflowing joy or out of frustration and disappointment? To me this is the most important theological question of them all, because the answer takes us to the very heart of God. If there hadn't been a fall, would Jesus still have come?

The answer is, yes yes yes. Yes, Jesus would have come if humanity had not rejected God. Because God's whole life has been shaped to be in relationship with us. God determined, from before the foundation of the universe, never to be – except to be in relationship with us. The incarnation comes out of the abundance of God, not out of the weakness of humanity. Jesus isn't some kind of hand grenade God lobbed into the earth's atmosphere to make an explosion of love, joy, peace, forgiveness and eternal life. Jesus isn't a device. Jesus isn't just a solution to a problem. Jesus isn't simply a piece of divine technology that backs up our hard drive when we crash. Jesus is the embodiment of there being nothing in God that is not committed to be in relationship to us, whatever the cost, and there being nothing in us that isn't made for relationship with God. Jesus is what we were really made for and what God is really all about.

Round about the beginning of December, people stop talking about the economy and the football for a moment and feel bold enough to ask each other a really personal question. 'Where are you planning on being for Christmas this year?' Of course they don't think of it as a personal question. It sounds like just a request for information, as in fact all personal questions do. And we hide the personal dimension behind mundane inquiries about the best route to Lancashire and whether it's worth getting the train. But the reason it's personal is that Christmas involves a lot of sitting around doing not much, a bit of cooking, a bit of walking, a bit of playing games, a bit of just being together. Things we don't do much of the rest of the year. You can't hide behind email and getting ready for work next day because there isn't any email and there isn't any work next day. So you'd better make sure the people you're spending Christmas with are people you can just hang around with. In fact, saying 'I want to spend Christmas with you' is saying to someone 'I don't see you as work or as some kind of means to an end: I see you as someone I just want to be with for your own sake. I want to be with you even if we're hanging around doing not much.' It's probably the least intense way of saying I love you. Chances are the people you spend Christmas with are people you deeply love, even if you maybe don't put it into words very often. Not necessarily admire, not necessarily are attracted to, not necessarily find easy, not necessarily agree with on their choice of spouse or on your parenting technique, but nonetheless people you just want to be with and enjoy for their humanity and for the glimpse of divinity you see in them.

It's the simplicity and humanity of these relationships, not our great achievements, that characterize our true identity. Because this is the way God loves us. We are not God's achievement. We are not a project God is constantly tinkering with in the garage till we're right. We are simply the ones with whom God wants to share life. God doesn't have a working relationship with us. God and humanity are not on a professional footing. God wants to spend Christmas with us – because God's whole life is shaped simply to be with us. Of course God wants us to kneel in faith and reverence, to order our lives as ones of righteousness and truth that issue in deeds of transparent kindness and costly generosity. But even if we don't, God loves us anyway. That's what Christmas shows us once and for all. And the way to celebrate Christmas is to love God back – not for what we've been given, for life and eternal life, for forgiveness and healing and hope and salvation, not out of gratitude or fear or admiration or wonder, but simply for God's own sake, the same way God loves us.

So when there's a great commotion in the control room and a jumpy data analyst holds out a trembling hand and points a nervous finger and says, 'See, there. That … that thing. We don't know what it is. We've done all the checks, captain, but there's no record of anything like this. It's alive. But it's like nothing this planet has ever seen before', what there's never been before isn't just a unique divine-human phenomenon, two natures in one person. What there's never been before is what's revealed in Jesus: the news that God's whole life is shaped to be in relationship with us and that God's chosen to draw us into that relationship not by force, not by guilt, not by threat, not by necessity, but by beauty, by joy, by the winsome simplicity and vulnerability and magnetism of a tiny child. That's why Christmas is the focal point of every year: because in this manger, in this baby, in this divine yet human flesh, we see God's determination to be with us forever, come what may. That's the heart of it all.

More than words

If you've ever seen *Fawlty Towers*, you'll know that it's basically one joke stretched out over twelve episodes. Basil Fawlty's the proprietor of an undistinguished hotel in Torquay. He's surrounded by imbeciles, in the form of some of his staff and several of his guests; but he's also beholden to the wealthier of his guests for income, so he has to find a way to contain his barely suppressed rage, enough to be polite to his guests and communicate with his staff. His frequent attempts and consistent failures to do this constitute the endless repeated cycle of wild flailings and ultimately explosive violence that makes the series agonizing, hilarious and gripping viewing.

But here's a question: what if it weren't a comedy? What if *Fawlty Towers* were actually a profound portrayal of human life, in which communication is largely impossible and conventions of civility are always on the point of snapping, whereupon violence inevitably ensues? Think about what it feels like to try to communicate with something or someone that can't or won't receive your radar signals and send appropriate signals back. Like a relentless puppy that just won't calm down, or a youth group that won't listen to instructions or demands; like a terrorist who won't be reasonable, or a flatmate to whom it's like talking to a brick wall. In all these situations, scary as it is to say it, violence lurks just beneath the surface. Words aren't helping you. You're perilously close to turning into Basil Fawlty and catapulting to a place beyond words. Civilization is about finding and learning ways to resolve tension and conflict without violence. But sometimes the best of us can teeter towards becoming profoundly uncivilized.

Which is why some of the most moving stories are about how two people can make a journey from a stand-off of frustrated and scarcely suppressed violence to a relationship of genuine peace. Virginia Axline was a primary school teacher in 1950s Ohio who went back to college and studied with the psychologist Carl Rogers. She developed the practice of child-centred play therapy, which offers warm, non-judgemental acceptance to children and patiently allows them to find their own solutions at their own pace. In a famous book, she describes a single child named Dibs, who presents as seldom speaking, often withdrawing, and frequently violently lashing out. Over the course of a year, by listening and not judging, Axline induces Dibs to find words for his feelings and begin to interact with his family and peers. She never asks questions like, 'Did you have a good time?' because they require a particular answer, which can leave a child trapped. She never says, 'See you next week', because she won't make promises that might not be kept. Gradually, trust and space and permission develop, and eventually the words emerge and the violence ceases. The book is subtitled *In Search of Self*, but I'd call it *Establishing Relationship* or even *Finding Words*.

The first sentence of the most important story ever written is this: 'In the beginning was the Word.' This sentence is itself a nod to the first sentence in the Bible, which starts, 'When all things began.' But it's saying something more profound than that earlier sentence. It's saying that communication – the desire to share and relate, the urge to engage and listen and receive and open up – is at the very core of all things, indeed the reason for the creation of all things. 'The Word was with God, and the Word was God.' That is to say, the essence that created existence, the forever that conceived of time, the everywhere that brought about here, is, at its very heart, about communication – nonviolent communication, partnership, relationship, togetherness. In fact, that's the purpose of existence – to communicate fully with one another and to communicate back with God. There's nothing more important than that.

But here we run into two problems. The first is, not all communication is healthy – some words are hurtful, cruel and destructive. (And you might not know this, but this was true even before the invention of Twitter.) The second is, words are sometimes only words. Words aren't always rooted in feelings, actions or integrity; sometimes words can be so far from actuality that they might just as well be called lies. In 1990 the rock band Extreme released a ballad that struck a chord with many people whose partners were quick with the terms of endearment, but whose way of showing it made those words empty. The song says that the words 'I love you' are not enough – what the singer wants is evidence of that love, what the singer calls 'more than words', because if the singer could see and feel and know that the love was real, then the partner wouldn't have to say 'I love you,' because, as the singer says, 'I'd already know.' Rock ballads don't get more searing than that.

Now I don't know anything about the religious persuasion of the members of Extreme, but I wonder if they've realized, all the thousands of times they've been called upon to sing their most famous song these last 30 years, that they are perfectly expressing the heart of what Christmas is all about. Let me set out the sequence as we've discovered it. Communication is at the heart of all things, because the real big bang that started this whole thing off was God's decision to be in relationship – for the persons of the Trinity to communicate as fully beyond themselves as they do with each other. Humanity is the purpose of creation, because humanity is the partner with whom God can be fully in relationship. But it turns out that humanity finds ways to twist communication from its created purpose as the texture of relationship to a sinister parody of relationship in cruelty and the outright undermining of relationship in lies. There's no Virginia Axline to come alongside wounded, fearful and withdrawn humanity and create trust through patience and understanding. Many prophets offer words; many brave souls offer examples. But collectively, humanity's response to God embodies the sentiment of that song: if you want it to be real, it's going to take more than words.

Which brings us to the most significant sentence in the Bible, and I would suggest the most important sentence ever written. A sentence about communication and how communication turns into trust and relationship. Fourteen verses into that same story I referred to earlier, a story known as John's Gospel, we find these priceless, peerless, perfect words: 'And the Word became flesh, and lived among us.' Here lies the fulfilment of the whole reason for the existence of all things. Everything that happened before this moment is backdrop and preparation. Everything that's happened since has been echo and embedding. This is the central moment, in which God's original desire to be with us becomes *more than words*. Jesus appears, fully human – born of a human mother in pretty desperate, shoddy, forsaken, neglected, rough and inhospitable conditions; let's just say the ox wasn't too particular where it went to the bathroom and the ass wasn't too fussed about where it brought up last night's fodder. But Jesus is also fully divine, for the heavens ring with the song of angels and a star guides the magi to the place of his birth. Jesus is the perfect communication of God to us, more than words; and Jesus is the perfect communication of us to God, showing God how we feel.

The whole of Jesus' life is like Virginia Axline's year with young Dibs. Jesus is creating an environment for us where we can live beyond cruelty and lies and finally find ways to dwell beyond violence in patience, understanding and trust. He's in search of our self, listening, not judging, offering open enquiry not closed questions, inviting us to wonder and discover and allowing us to find our own solutions at our own pace. Jesus is the Word of God that offers us the epitome of communication, through which we may find a relationship that lasts forever.

Yet there's no naïveté in Christmas. There's simplicity and a degree of innocence – but no naïveté. Because we all know that cruelty and lies enter Christ's story soon enough. They're there in Herod's court when the magi go to Jerusalem by mistake, and they're there when Herod sends soldiers to kill all the young children in Bethlehem. And they catch up with Jesus in the end, when his communication meets the world's violence and for a moment violence prevails. But the light of communication and relationship shines in the darkness of violence, and promises that, if we can only find time and patience, we will eventually see trust and relationship emerge from even the most violent of our failures to find words.

This is the wonder of Christmas. *The Word becomes more than words.* And inspires us to let the Holy Spirit of patience and tenderness turn our own violent frustration and anger into relationship and trust, and eventually to let those words become flesh, in embodied gestures and commitments of solidarity and love. It's because the Word became flesh, because God came among us to embody utter relationship with us, because God has faced the worst of our cruelty and lies, because God has shown us, because God has made it real, that we gather this holy night, with stars so brightly shining, and say to God, boldly, bravely, gladly, 'You don't have to say that you love us – because we already know.'

PART 2

Easter

4

Early on the First Day of the Week: Reflections on Easter Morning

Why are you crying?

I wonder if you've ever looked into a deep, dark cave. It's cold, it's mysterious, it's maybe a little damp, and there's this little voice in your head that's saying to you, 'If I go down too far into it either there'll be something scary and angry down there that'll get me, or maybe worse, there'll be some kind of rock that will roll across the face of the cave and shut me in – and no one will hear my cries.'

Mary Magdalene was looking into a cave like that on the first Easter morning. And it turned out there were indeed some creatures in the dark cave. Two angels. So not your average tomb, then. The angels are pretty observant, mind you. They can see the state Mary's in. They say to her, 'Why are you crying?' You can tell these angels have never done a course in pastoral care and counselling. Because the first thing you learn in pastoral care and counselling is, 'Never ask, "Why?"' 'Why?' is a useless question. It's threatening, unsupportive, paralysing and conversation-stopping. It's almost certain to make the person cry all the more, because if they could give a satisfactory answer they probably wouldn't be crying, stupid. Mary, to her credit, doesn't say, 'That's not a very helpful question. What kind of an angel are you?' She says, 'They've taken away my Lord, and I don't know where they've laid him.'

Let's put ourselves in Mary's shoes for a moment and allow ourselves to be asked that question. 'Why are you crying?' Why is Mary crying? Let's hear her answer. 'I'm crying because I'm experiencing horrifying loss, aching grief and a huge hole where the love and hope and trust and joy of my life used to be. This man, this more-than-just-a-man, who was supposed to be laid in this tomb, turned my life from monochrome to technicolour, from a lonely violin to a crescendoing orchestra, from a limp and falling feather to a soaring eagle's wing. I'm crying because I'm staring into the horror of death, and death right now seems to be obliterating everything I want, everything I need, everything I know. I feel so powerless, so fragile, so alone.'

But perhaps if we asked a more thoughtful question, we'd get an even bigger answer. 'What's going through your mind, Mary?' Then she might say, 'I keep thinking of the way they killed him. The nails, the blood, the jeering laughter, the noise, the sneering, the baying for blood, the throwing dice, the cheering, the way the disciples all ran away, the way Pilate washed his hands, the finger-pointing, the lashing, the spear piercing his side. Human beings can be so cruel, so mean, so violent, so stupid, so weak, so selfish, so treacherous. It's not just the death that makes me cry; it's the sin.'

And then maybe we'd ask a deeper question and we'd get a bigger answer still. 'Mary, what d'you think God makes of your tears?' I wonder if she'd say, 'I think God's crying too. That's what makes my tears feel right. I feel I'm weeping with God's tears. Who can bear to see God's tears? I feel by letting myself cry I'm sharing in God's tears, mingling my tears with the tears of the Father, who's grieving the death of Jesus and mortified by the depth of our sin. Somehow in these tears I feel I'm alone with the aloneness of God.'

Here's Mary, staring into the unknown, weeping. And she's asked the question, 'Why are you crying?' And her answer is, because of death, because of sin, because God's crying too.

And that leads me to ask the same Easter morning question of you, as you look into the unknown. 'Why are you crying?' Of course we've all got resistances to answering the question. We've erected a wall of privacy around us, we've drawn a curtain of self-sufficiency, we've established a demeanour of emotional steadiness. 'I'm not crying,' we say. 'I'm not the crying type.' But then we look at Mary, as she has the courage to stare into the nothingness of the tomb, and we begin to touch the territory of those trembling tears.

'I'm crying because I realize my life is an orchestrated denial of death, and someday I'm going to have to face the truth of my mortality. I'm crying because like Mary I've lost people who put the colour in my rainbow and wind beneath my wings. I'm crying because I've been hurt and disappointed and betrayed, and I'm bleeding with pain about these things. But I'm also crying because I've been no angel myself, and I've done some things I can't undo, and I'm part of some habits and systems and addictions I can't extricate myself from, and I can't bear to see the pain I've caused others. I'm crying because I want to have a faith that takes the grief away but somehow I seem to find that being with God makes me cry more, not less. I'm crying because I'm just overwhelmed.' Is that why you're crying?

Let me tell you about one night when I was crying. It was Christmas Eve, around 15 years ago. I was a young pastor. (I like to think I'm still a young pastor.) A few months earlier I'd been appointed to a church on the edge of town whose Sunday morning congregation was about 15. We started making plans for Christmas. We made a leaflet with a wise and witty Christmas message and a list of all the Christmas worship services on it. I insisted there should be a Midnight Communion. That was always the highlight of my Christmas growing up. No one in the congregation remembered ever going to church at midnight, but I still thought it was a great idea. I set the time for 11.30 pm, 24 December. We organized. We leafleted the whole neighbourhood – more than 3,000 houses. 11pm Christmas Eve came. No one there. 11.15 ... still no one there. 11.25 ... still just me, the bread, and the wine. 11.30 ... I tried so hard, so hard, to stop a tear beginning to roll down my eyelashes.

Why was I crying? Because I'd tried so hard. Because for a moment I'd dared to hope. Because I felt I'd failed. Because I wondered if the church was dying. Because I felt humiliated.

I heard a rustling noise. I looked at my watch. It was 11.32. The door opened. Into the church walked a man and a woman, maybe late forties. I'd never seen them before. 'Is it just us?' they asked. 'I'm afraid it is,' I replied, wondering if they were going to laugh at me. 'Oh good,' the woman said. 'We waited outside in the garden to see if anyone else would come, and when we thought we'd be the only ones, we walked in.' 'How d'you mean,' I said, gesturing them to sit down. After all, who wants to be alone at midnight on Christmas Eve with a hopelessly underachieving pastor? 'Well,' she said, 'I guess you should know that Dave and I used to be married to other people until recently. There's a lot of folk unhappy about us being together. We moved out here because we didn't feel we could go to any of the downtown churches. In fact, we haven't been to church at all for over a year. We were frightened to come tonight, but when we saw we'd be the only ones, we got the courage to walk through the door. Our lives are a mixture of love and shame. We want to begin again.'

I stared at them in silence for a long time. It was a man and a woman in a garden. It was a story of death and fear and sin and shame and tears; and beginning and life and trust and change and love. It was midnight on Christmas Eve. But, through my tears, I was staring at the dawn of Easter Day. By the end of that night, I was still crying. But I was crying a different kind of tears. I was crying Easter tears.

When Mary turns away from the tomb, having not got much change out of the angels, she begins another conversation, this time with a man she takes to be the gardener, but we realize to be someone else. Jesus asks Mary the same question the angels just asked her. 'Why are you crying?' He clearly hasn't done the pastoral care and counselling course either. And unless he wasn't paying attention, he must have heard the answer she gave to the angels. But Jesus adds a second question. 'Whom are you looking for?'

'Whom are you looking for?' Now that is a good question. That's a good question to ask anyone, and it's an especially good question to ask Mary right this minute. Because Mary's obviously looking for Jesus. But who is Jesus? Well, here's the crucial point. The story has shown us who Jesus is. Remember

why Mary was crying? Mary was crying because she was facing her sense of loss in the face of death, her sense of fragility
and weakness and loneliness and powerlessness. This is who
Jesus is. He's the one who overcomes death and transforms the
fragile, the weak, the lonely and the powerless. Staring into the
tomb she began to realize whom she is looking for.

But there's more. Who is Jesus? Mary was crying because
she'd seen how ghastly humankind can be, she'd witnessed
brutality and horror and duplicity and killing and betrayal.
This is who Jesus is. He's the one who dismantles sin, deflates
enmity, heals cruelty, absorbs malice, forgives treachery. Staring
into the tomb Mary begins to realize whom she is looking for.

There's still more. Who is Jesus? Mary was crying because
she was shedding God's tears, tears of sadness for God's separation from us, from the rebellious creation. This is who Jesus
is. He's the one who reunites us with God. He's the one who
blends our tears with God's tears, he's the good shepherd who
knows each one of us by name and gathers us into the Father's
sheepfold, he's the true vine who grafts each one of us on as his
branches. Staring into the tomb Mary begins to realize whom
she is looking for.

And then Jesus says one word. 'Mary.' When you've been
crying, what's the most helpful thing anyone can do? They can
be silent with you, in wordless presence, to affirm the value of
your sorrow and the truth of your tears. They can touch you,
gently, respectfully, lovingly, to share your humanity and show
you you're not alone. And they can speak tenderly, just a word
or two, that makes you feel accompanied, received, understood.

'Mary.' She's crying, but she feels the sense of a companion
with whom she will never again be alone, she senses the touch
of the one who will never let her go, she hears her name like
never before. 'Mary.' Her eyes are opened. She's looking into
the face of the resurrected Jesus.

And now, surely, she discovers a different kind of tears. She's
known what it means to be overwhelmed by loss, by sin, by
the absence of God. But now she's crying more than ever, yet
in a new way. She's crying because, if Jesus has emerged from

the tomb, that means he's not been destroyed by the grave, and she's blinded by the wonder of imagining what it's like to live beyond death, to enjoy life forever, to put aside fear and loss and grief and sorrow; and the tears are cascading down her cheeks and falling to the ground in fountains of joy. She's crying because, if Jesus is alive, that means he's dismantled sin, and she's swathed in a shower of tears in dreaming of a world where enmity's healed, hatred is transformed, cruelty is turned to kindness and anger is displaced by mercy. She's crying because if Jesus is looking at her that means he's reunited us with God, and her disbelief is being washed away by a tidal wave of grace, and she's in an ocean of glory with angels and archangels and saints and cherubim and all the company of heaven. These tears don't seek the comfort of one person to share, to receive, to cherish and to understand. These tears are infectious – they need to be taken to the whole world. These are the tears of baptism that are sent to refresh everyone; this is an overwhelming that's destined to flood the whole creation with joy. Mary's asking the whole creation, 'Why aren't you crying?'

Here are a man and a woman in a garden, the very picture that started the whole Bible, the very place where everything went wrong. And here again is this man and this woman, at the very place where everything is put right again; but way beyond the imagination of that first man and woman, because here is not just the setting-right of human relations with one another, but here is the reunion between humanity, creation and God. If that doesn't make you cry with tears of joy, nothing ever will.

So here's my Easter morning question for you Why are you crying? Are you looking into the tomb, overwhelmed by grief, by sin, by utter loneliness? Or are you looking into the face of the risen Lord, overwhelmed by glory, by wonder, by joy? Whom are you looking for? The one who overcomes death, dismantles sin and reunites you with God? Well, here's the good news of Easter. God's looking at you, kid.

Easter's drenched in tears. But they're tears of joy.

Touch and go

A few days ago, I got a call from a friend. As soon as I heard her voice I knew things weren't right. 'Where are you?' I said. 'Just round the corner from St Martin's', she said. 'Let's do this face-to-face', I said, and five minutes later she was sitting in front of me. 'It feels like it's all fallen apart', she said. 'All the work I've done over the last few years, everything I've hoped and planned for. It's just gone south.' And she stared at the floor. She stared at the floor for a long time. We both did. Not because the floor had a lot of answers, but probably because if she'd looked any-where else she'd have started to cry and she didn't want to do that – probably because if she started she didn't know when she'd stop.

After we said goodbye, I picked up John chapter 20 and I realized who she was and what she'd been looking at, in that long, disbelieving, crushed and demoralised gaze at the floor. She was Mary Magdalene and she'd been looking deep into the darkness of the empty tomb. Mary's staring into the tomb because the tomb is the closest she can get to Jesus; the Jesus who'd called her, restored her, given her life meaning and pur-pose, taken her seriously, offered her a future and a hope – the Jesus who'd more or less created her. And he was gone – not just gone, but destroyed; not just destroyed, but humiliated, expunged and obliterated. And everything he stood for – for-giveness, justice, freedom, everlasting life, empowerment, glory, truth – it was all vaporized with him. And to add insult to injury, now his dead body was gone too.

This moment is even worse than Good Friday. Good Friday has sacrifice, nobility, dedication, a macabre beauty. But this moment, as Mary gazes into the heart of darkness, there's noth-ing to see but waste, indignity, horror, loss, cruelty, disgrace, despair. It's not that there isn't wonder and life – this is after all a garden, morning has broken, the world's waking up, there's creativity and action and energy all around. But Mary's look-ing deep into where it all ends, the tomb of death that makes a mockery of the ephemeral parade of life, a plughole that drags all creation down into a vortex of spiralling desolation. This is the paradox of life, right here: the wonder of fertile, vibrant creation, and the everlasting darkness of doomed death. Which one is ultimately the truth? Mary at this moment thinks she's just found out. And she's weeping uncontrollable tears.

But listen. This instant of total dejection is when she hears one single word. Her own name. 'Mary'. When Christians use the phrase 'the word of God', sometimes they mean the Bible, sometimes they refer to the preached or proclaimed word of the gospel, sometimes they're talking about Jesus the logic of God made flesh. But this moment encapsulates every meaning of 'the word'. Mary's looking deep and far into the horror of a world without God, and then she hears the word – one single word that changes everything. One single word turns death to life, despair to hope, darkness to light. Mary. 'I am the good shepherd', he'd said, 'and I call my sheep by name.' Mary.

Mary doesn't figure any of this out for herself. For a while she's so overwhelmed and preoccupied with the black hole of despond that she can't make out any other reality. But then she does the simplest, humblest, most straightforward, yet most crucial and transformative thing of her whole life: she turns round. And in that turning we see the whole gospel. Jesus calls us by name. Jesus is Adam, the first man, meeting Eve in the garden and saying 'Could we start again please?' Jesus is Abraham, the embodiment of Israel, meeting Sarah and saying, 'Could we go on a new journey and become a true blessing to the whole world?' Jesus is Moses, the liberator, meeting Miriam and saying, 'Could we begin our long walk to freedom?' Mary turns from horror to elation, from depression to joy, from abyss to glory. A moment ago, death engulfed everything. Now Mary's inhabiting a story of beginnings, blessings and belongings. It takes one word. The word of God.

And what does Mary do? She reaches out to embrace the risen Jesus. Of course she does. She celebrates, she rejoices, she shares the wonder. Think about every embrace you've ever known: the cuddle of a child, the reassurance of a friend, the greeting of a companion, the ecstasy of a lover, the consolation of a sympathizer, the strength of a rescuer. This is the definitive embrace of all time: Mary meets her maker, her redeemer, her empowerer. If you want to know what heaven feels like, this is it: sorrow turns to dancing, words turn to song, death turns to life. Every time we hug someone we're reminding them of this most important hug of all. This is the touch of life, hope in the face of death, solidarity in the midst of bewilderment, reunion after trauma, tenderness overcoming isolation.

But an embrace isn't all that Jesus has in store for Mary, or in store for us. Here are the hardest words in the Easter story: 'Don't keep hold of me.' I wonder if you've ever hugged some-one and never wanted to let go. You want to keep that moment forever, treasure that touch and inscribe it on your heart, retain that love and be fed by it every moment. But ponder that feel-ing for a moment. However wonderful it is, doesn't the desire to preserve that embrace ultimately reduce the other person to an instrument of your own needs? Isn't there more to their life than making you feel cherished and beloved? Jesus says to Mary, 'I love you totally and have been raised to restore you to life and be with you forever; but I am also here for everyone else – I'm not just your toy – and most of all I'm here to restore the dance of the Holy Trinity that's the essence of all things. Don't confuse the beginning of the gospel with the whole of salvation; don't reduce love to the intensity of the moment; don't restrict the glory to just you and me.'

Quickly Mary discovers what it is that's so wonderful that it's worth interrupting an embrace with the risen Jesus. Again, it's all in one word: 'Go'. Just as the whole of the gospel is contained in that single word, 'Mary', so the whole of ministry and mission is encapsulated in that single word, 'Go'. Mary was powerless, pitiful and dejected, and now she's purposeful, focused and energized. Her task is to tell – she has news, she's seen the glory, she has truth to share. And she's going to the people Jesus calls 'my brothers' – that is, those who betrayed him not two days ago; the fact that he calls them 'brothers' means this is news of forgiveness as well as resurrection. The news is that Jesus is ascending, in other words that her Lord is the Lord of heaven and earth, that the intensity and passion and devotion of her relationship with Jesus is replicated in God's passion and devotion towards her. The resurrection, the forgiveness and the everlasting life God has given to Jesus, God is longing to give to her and to her brothers, those who've betrayed and denied and forsaken and fled.

So here are the three Easter words. Turn – from despair to joy. Touch – but know when to let go. And Go – because there's new life to live, news to share, restoration to embody. Turn. Touch. Go.

I wonder if you know what it feels like to stare at the floor like my friend last week. I wonder if that's how you have been feeling recently. I wonder which of those three Easter words you find the hardest. To turn – to realize that despair and despondency aren't the last word, that by being absorbed by them you're missing the gentle presence behind you. To touch – to see that your longing to be held, loved, embraced, met is only part of your deeper calling to share the joy of God with all God's children. To go – to find life in good work, bring reconciliation and healing and truth and discovery to those who're beset by grief and regret and bitterness and hurt.

Turn. Touch. Go. The three Easter words. And they start with a woman looking deep into the heart of darkness, believing all is lost and meaningless and ruined and rotten. Jesus is back. Death can't hold him. He's come back for you. He's come back to embrace you. He's come back to give you good work to do, with him, forever. Turn and greet him. He's calling your name.

Whom are you looking for?

In the Middle Ages, a central motif around which people conceived their lives was that of the quest. The notion of pilgrimage captured people's sense of the unfinished, transitory nature of existence and the search for truth. The quest shaped people's notions of romance, of faith and of honour – the whole idea of the Crusades came about in blending the pilgrimage to Jerusalem with the challenge to regain the holy places for Christendom. And the key to the quest is that you discover as much about yourself and your destination on the journey as you do on reaching your goal. We understand the same principle today, whether we're going on a school trip to the Eden Project or making a parish pilgrimage to Iona. The destination is a focus but it's just as much about what you learn about God, yourself and your companions on the way.

I want you to think of John's Gospel as a quest. Its climax is Jesus' resurrection. But just as important is what we learn on the way; because what we learn on the way teaches us what resurrection means. The clue to this lies in the first thing Jesus says after his resurrection. 'Who are you looking for?' If you look back to the very first thing Jesus says in this gospel, it's more or less the same question: 'What are you looking for?' The implication is that between the beginning and the end of the story we've learnt the answer to that question. The difference between the two questions is that the first one makes us look back over the Old Testament to see what it's really all about, whereas the second question makes us look back over the gospel to find out what's different about Jesus.

The Old Testament is about the interweaving of two themes. The first is covenant. The epicentre of the Old Testament is the giving of the Law to Moses at Sinai. Everything that goes before that moment, including the liberation from slavery and the exodus from Egypt, is a preparation for it, and everything that comes after, including entering the Promised Land and the coming of the kings, is part of the great quest to discover whether and how long Israel can keep its covenant with God. The second theme is creation. The great discovery of Israel's time in exile in Babylon is that the God who'd liberated them from slavery in Egypt was the same God who'd made heaven and earth. This is the centre of our faith – that God almighty, the creator, astonishingly wants to be in relationship with us, tucked away in this little corner of the universe; and at the same time that our longing to be in relationship and find meaning and truth in our paltry existence is met by none other than the power that created, sustains and will bring to an end all things.

And John's story of Easter is constructed around these two themes, covenant and creation. When Mary looks into the tomb, what she sees is two angels sitting where Jesus' body had lain, one at the head and the other at the feet. It's a perfect echo of the description of the mercy seat, the ark of the covenant that contained the ten commandments, as described in Exodus chapter 25. In other words, God's covenant with Israel is fulfilled in the risen Jesus. God has not left us – even after the worst possible breaking of the covenant, the killing of God's only son, the covenant can yet survive. And then when Mary looks round from the tomb, she sees what she takes to be the gardener. It *is* the gardener – the one who created the garden. We have a man and a woman in a garden, on the first day of the week: and it's evidently a fulfilment of the creation story. So in the climax of John's Gospel, we have the fulfilment of everything the Old Testament was about – covenant and creation.

And when we put that together with the question Jesus is asking at the outset of John's gospel, we've solved our riddle. Jesus says, 'What are you looking for?' The first disciples, on behalf of Israel, are bewailing the desperate state of God's people and are looking for a restoration of the covenant by the creator God who made heaven and earth. And everything Jesus does in the course of John's Gospel is demonstrating – by his restoration of relationships and his power over food and eyesight and seas and wind and finally death – that he is the re-creating God who can restore the covenant. And here in the resurrection we find the consummation of that restored covenant and renewed creation in the new mercy seat and the new garden of Eden. Jesus is everything Israel was looking for.

Who are you looking for? If you look back on your whole life as a quest, what are the constant themes? And in what ways are you looking for a person or an event to unlock the riddle and disclose the secret?

Who are you looking for? The gospel story is saying to you, on Easter Day, 'I think I know what you're looking for. You're looking for forgiveness, reconciliation, and a new relationship with God. And you're looking for a renewed world and a world in tune and at peace with God forever.' And on Easter Day we discover that these aren't ideals in a fantasy, or proposals in a manifesto, or lyrics in a song. They're a person, a person standing before Mary saying, 'I am renewed covenant and new creation. I am everything Israel was looking for and everything the world right now needs. I am what you've walked the world over searching for and everything God wants to give you.'

And there's one thing more. One secret beyond even this. All the time we thought it was *our* quest, our searching, our journeying, our discovery. But there's a bigger quest than our quest. If we dare face the risen Lord on Easter Day, and if we dare ask Jesus the same question he asks us, we will get the greatest reward of all. We will look into the face of our risen Jesus and say, 'Lord of creation and covenant, all these years, since the foundation of the world, all this suffering, all this mystery, all this waiting, all this long, long detour through the wilderness. Who've you been looking for?' And he'll reply, with tears in his eyes, 'I've been looking for you.'

The secret garden

I wonder whether you've ever had a secret rendezvous. It's the kind of thing that makes you whisper for fear of being found out, or shiver with suppressed excitement. A phone call, an email or a text message says 'Meet me tonight at 6. You're the only person who can help me'; or 'I've got something I need to tell you'; or even 'I just can't go another day without seeing you.' You're breathless, your heart's pounding, and you're overcome with impatient curiosity and furtive intrigue.

Easter's about not just one secret rendezvous, but a whole series, all taking place at the same time. And they all take place in a garden. One book in the Bible has a number of references to secret meetings in a garden. And that book is the Song of Songs. The Song of Songs is about erotic love, about a physical, intimate, passionate embrace between two people whose lovemaking is a kind of worship of God. In the coming together of two lovers, the Song of Songs invites us to see that God's deepest desire is for us and our deepest desire is for God. There's a reason why the Song of Songs is particularly significant. Jesus' death took place at Passover. At each of their five great festivals the Jews read one of the shorter Old Testament books, known as the Scrolls. The scroll they read at Passover is the Song of Songs. And repeatedly the Song of Songs refers to a garden, and represents the garden as a place of secret rendezvous and fertile growth.

In the Middle East, gardens aren't very common. They're very special. The climate is dry, the ground is dusty, rain can be rare. In Arabic the word 'garden' has a particular resonance. The Arabic word for 'garden' is 'paradise'. That's where the whole notion of paradise comes from. Paradise means flowing water in a desert, green shoots in dry ground, lush beauty in the midst of arid wastelands. Easter is a glimpse into paradise, because the Easter story shows us a series of wondrous meetings all taking place in a secret garden one special morning.

Let's look at the first rendezvous. Easter is the moment when the beginning meets the end. At the start of the Bible there's a man and a woman in a garden. Adam and Eve. Intimacy and destiny. All of creation focused in this one relationship. And at the end there's another encounter in a garden. This time it's God and his bride the church coming down from heaven as the new Jerusalem, in a garden where the leaves on the trees are for the healing of the nations. And now here, on Easter morning, Jesus meets Mary Magdalene, a man meets a woman, in a garden. Beginning meets end, creation meets completion right here in this resurrection garden. Resurrection shows us the *last* page of the story, how things will be for all time; but it also shows us the *first* page of the story, by placing a man and a woman in a garden, just like in Genesis. Here, in this garden, in the meeting of this man and woman, the beginning and end of all things meet. The resurrection of Jesus is the end of the beginning and it's the beginning of the end. It's the central moment of history. That's quite a big secret. Whisper it if you dare.

And there's more. Easter's the moment when the body meets the soul. We're used to controversy between religion and science. We're used to science saying we're just fragile physical bodies with predictable behaviours and religion saying we're really immortal souls with a God-given identity. But the resurrection of Jesus cuts through this debate. Here is Jesus, utterly physical, scarred and defeated by the agony of crucifixion, and now so real before Mary that she clings on to him for all she's worth. He's not an intangible soul – he's the most real and physical thing she's ever felt and touched. And yet he's the most holy thing too. Easter is a reaffirmation of Christmas: the resurrection is a reaffirmation of the incarnation. God's not above and beyond flesh and blood – God's a reality *in* flesh and blood, now and forever. This is the central moment of history, and what we see in Jesus is the resurrection body, fully human, fully physical, fully infused with the spirit of God. The old idea that the body tied us to earth and the soul tied us to God has gone. Here in the risen Lord heaven and earth are united as never before. Here we see the destiny for our bodies and souls: to be remade beyond death as people soaked in humanity and immersed in God. Easter's the day we glimpse eternity. That's quite a big secret. Whisper it if you dare.

But there's even more. Easter's the moment when the personal meets the social. When we think about dying maybe our deepest fear is not pain or even oblivion, but fundamentally being eternally alone. Never to wake up seems terrifying. But one day to wake up and be eternally alone seems even worse. Death seems the most isolating experience imaginable. But here in the garden Jesus' resurrection isn't something for him alone. He shares it with Mary. He tenderly speaks her name. When we deeply love someone, we're terrified that our bodily limitations, our other commitments and our impending deaths mean we can't be truly, intimately, everlastingly as one with them as we yearn to be. But here's Jesus, once dead now risen, truly, intimately, everlastingly with Mary. And not just with Mary, but with the people he calls the 'brothers'. The mystery of love is how we can love one person so much and yet still love others too. Here, that mystery's solved. God in the risen Christ loves us all, but loves each one of us as if we were the only one. And once again the garden's crucial. Here the garden is telling us that resurrection is not just intimate, not just social, but also cosmic. It's for all creation. The garden represents the whole non-human creation. Just as Adam and Eve were the focal point for the destiny and fall of all things, so this secret meeting between Jesus and Mary is the focal point for the resurrection of all things. Easter is when the personal meets the social, the social meets the cosmic, and Jesus is all in all. This is a picture of everlasting life with God. That's another very big secret. Whisper it if you dare.

Here we have a series of meetings in a secret garden. Each meeting is about one and the same thing. And that thing is the best news and the biggest secret in the world: the fulfilment of God's deep desire for us and the fulfilment of our deep desire for God. These meetings are showing us what's meant by paradise.

One kind of theatre that never goes out of fashion is farce. Here's the scene that everybody loves. We get three subplots which all reach their climax at the same time. In the first there's two characters called the beginning and the end. In the second there's two characters called the body and the soul. In the third there's two characters called the personal and the social. It turns out that they've each made separate secret arrangements to meet by the large rock in the garden near Golgotha early on Sunday morning. The audience realizes that all six characters are going to show up at the same place at the same time, but in a farce the characters don't know what the audience knows. Most likely they each walk slowly and secretively backwards toward each other and if you want to ham it up you have piano notes that go du ... du ... du ... du ... doooo-duh-duh-duh-duh ... until they all bump backsides and jump into the air. It's the kind of thing it's hilarious to watch over and over again because each time you not only laugh at the characters, but you also more deeply appreciate their interconnections and the intricacies of the plot that brought them all there.

And this meeting in the garden between Mary Magdalene and

Jesus is a lot like farce. It's a simultaneous secret rendezvous between beginning and end, between body and soul, between person and society. You can see Mary backing slowly away from the tomb and bumping into a man she takes to be the gardener. She's so blinded by grief she stupidly thinks he's the gardener! But the whole point is, he *is* the gardener! He's the Lord who'd made the Garden of Eden, who'd opened up creation as a playground of delights. This is the reunion of creation and final destiny, and in the clumsiness of her grief Mary's stumbled into it.

Meanwhile Mary's still peering into the empty tomb. She's still living in a world where body is separated from soul. She's looking at the empty place where the dead body ought to be and she's backing away from it ... and though she knows she's bumped into a living person, it doesn't cross her mind it might be Jesus because she knows Jesus is dead and all she's hoping to find is his body. But the whole point is, this is the great reunion of body and soul, and she's about to be the first to witness it. And straightaway she grabs hold of Jesus, which means she gets the message that this really is God and this really is flesh and blood, so it's Christmas all over again, but even better this time because this time it's forever.

And then think again about the significance of the resurrection as an event both between Jesus and Mary and between Jesus and the brothers. Mary – isolated, grieving, captivated by death – the epitome of what it means to be lost – is walking backwards from the tomb in dismay ... when she's deeply met in the most tender way possible – by the good shepherd who knows her by name. 'Mary'. Jesus has made the long journey to all humanity to show us the face of God in spite of our sin, and now here he makes a special journey to show his risen face to just one of us, Mary, softly and tenderly. Because he sought out and met Mary, we have reason to hope that he'll do just the same to you and me. He died to save us all, but he makes a resurrection appearance to each one of us as if we were the only one.

I wonder if you have a secret garden. I wonder whether there are two irreconcilable commitments, two overlapping loves, two painfully separated poles in your life. And I wonder whether there may be a secret rendezvous in a garden, and while God is getting on with the business of bringing together personal and social, beginning and end, body and soul, God may be just as busy reconciling the contradictory extremes in your heart. I wonder if in Jesus' tender words of greeting and recognition, 'Mary', you hear a call to bring to harmony the discordant notes in your being. And if so, Easter morning may not just be a celebration of the way God resurrects all things, but even a celebration of the way God reconciles you.

Easter's about a garden. Easter's about the coming together of creation and destiny, body and soul, personal and social. Easter fulfils our desire for God and God's desire for us. And all of this is disclosed in an encounter between a man and a woman in a garden. A gentle presence, a gentle touch, a gentle word. This is eternal life. This is paradise.

5

I Have Seen the Lord:
Reflections on the Risen Christ

If Christ is risen

In his 1669 book, *Pensées*, or *Thoughts*, the French mathematician and philosopher Blaise Pascal posits the notion that 'if' is the most important word in history. He gives the example of Cleopatra's nose. Cleopatra was, he says, not only a political leader but also a great beauty; it was the combination of the two, epitomized by her large and authoritative nose, that entranced Mark Antony and Julius Caesar. If Mark Antony had not been so attracted to Cleopatra then it would not have set in train a sequence of events that divided the Roman leadership, brought about the Battle of Actium, led to Octavian becoming Emperor Augustus, and caused the end of the republic and the beginning of the Roman Empire. All because of a nose. All hanging on that tiny word, 'if'.

Pascal's thesis fell well out of fashion in the nineteenth century. Karl Marx believed that dialectical materialism controlled the destiny of events, and even his arch-opponents, the nationalists that reunified Italy and Germany, assumed there was an unseen force that guided history beyond the precarious power of the little word 'if'. The Cleopatra's nose theory of history was taken to be an exaggeration.

But I want to suggest to you that Pascal's mistake wasn't to exaggerate the power of the word 'if'. Pascal's mistake was to underestimate it. And to pick the wrong example. In fact, there's only one example that really matters. And that's the example we celebrate at Easter. Easter is about the biggest 'if' imaginable, the most precarious conditional clause in the universe. Paul puts it as bluntly as can be: 'If Christ has not been raised, your faith is futile', he says. 'If for this life only we have hoped in Christ, we are of all people most to be pitied.'

This is the 'if' on which all of reality hangs. If Christ is not risen, Christianity falls apart. Christmas shows us that God's whole being is shaped to be with us. The Trinity has a second person who is fully human as well as fully divine. We see that human face of God at Bethlehem. Good Friday shows us that in order to be with us, Christ will risk even his being with the Father – hence his words, 'My God, my God, why have you forsaken me?' And in order to let Jesus be with us, the Father is prepared to risk even his being with Christ. But then if Christ is not risen, the Trinity is in tatters. God, split apart by Good Friday, is shattered for good. God is in pieces, not temporarily, but permanently.

If Christ is not risen, death has the last word. All our gloomy fears that after our last breath there is nothing and we become as unconscious of reality as we were before we were born, are realized. If Christ is not risen, there's no hope for our future in God, there is no joy in life beyond what we can eke out in these three score years and ten; those who cling on to every last second of existence are probably right, life is but a walking shadow, a poor player that struts and frets his hour upon the stage and then is heard no more.

If Christ is not risen, sin is not overcome. The naked power that put Jesus to death, the betrayal of Judas, the denial of Peter, the handwashing of Pilate, the conniving of Caiaphas – all these things have no counterbalance. They sway the scales. The wondrous transformation of forgiveness, the final vindication of the just in the face of evil, the judgement in which every tear is dried and every broken heart made whole – all these things are wishful thinking. If Christ is not risen, all justice in the universe is a pious ideal, a railing against reality, a conviction without evidence.

If Christ is not risen, the Pharisees and Sadducees were right. Jesus was simply a Jewish man, his claims and others' projections about him were inflated and blasphemous, he was a wild prophet with a healing hand and a large ego. If Christ is not risen the gospels tell a faraway story of a wandering miracle-man with no great significance for today, except to illustrate that idealistic prophets usually come to a brutal end at the hands of ruthless regimes.

If Christ is not risen, the church is built on sand, and 2,000 years of hope turn to ashes. All that's left of the worldwide mission of the disciples is a bunch of nice classical music, a lot of kindness and mercy and some beautiful architecture. If Christ is not risen, and for this life only we have hoped, we are of all people most to be pitied. It's as bad as that.

But slowly turn around like Mary in the garden, stand stock-still like Paul on the road to Damascus, sit open-mouthed like the disciples in a locked room, stare into your supper like the companions en route to Emmaus. Sing hallelujah with the angels in heaven, jump from the boat like Peter on the Sea of Galilee, run headlong like the women from the tomb, say 'My Lord and my God' like Thomas in the upper room; dismantle all your ifs, put away your despair, be renewed in faith, hope and love: for Christ *is* risen. And now reassess everything in all creation because of this single, simple, but titanic discovery.

If Christ is risen Christianity suddenly makes sense. Christmas is God's desire to be with us: Easter is God's promise to be with us always. Good Friday is God's declaration that no sacrifice, not even putting the inner relationships of the Trinity in jeopardy, is too great to deter God's will to be with us; Easter is God's demonstration that neither sin nor death can finally separate us.

If Christ is risen death does not have the last word. Whether long like Simeon and Anna's, or short like that of Jesus and John the Baptist, our lives are simply a foretaste of what is to come, a trial run before the threshold of resurrection, an inkling of what lies in store in the life eternal. We live this life not pitifully trying to hoard and preserve and protect things we vainly hope we can keep forever, but freely sharing and giving and offering things we know we will be given back a hundredfold beyond the grave. Instead of making futile efforts to overcome the limitations of our lives and the mortality that circumscribes our existence, we look to our restored relationship with God and a power far stronger than the wastes of decay and the ravages of time.

If Christ is risen sin will not finally poison our souls. Every wrong step will be redeemed by forgiveness and healed by reconciliation. At Easter God has turned the worst that humanity can do in crucifying Jesus into the best that we could imagine in giving us life in divine relationship forever. Nothing will be beyond God's improvising grace to redeem and transform and make beautiful. Nothing at all. Every ghastly word, mean thought or dreadful deed that we have done or has been inflicted on us will be turned into glory. Evil will not just be defeated, it will be changed into good. Its acid rain will turn into fertilizer for God's kingdom.

If Christ is risen and the promises that Jesus made about his dying and rising have come true, we can trust his other promises, we can know he is who he said he was, we can be confident that his is a story with significance for the whole universe. This fragile tale of Abraham and Moses and David is indeed the soil in which God grows the redemption of the world. All other knowledge and history and science and philosophy may be valuable and helpful and honest and true; but only this one thing can save, can change everything, can be the particular story around which and from which all other stories find their meaning.

If Christ is risen the church is the frail, foolish and fallible bearer of the most wondrous, liberating and glorious news in the world. Every hapless, shameless or feckless thing the church gets wrong only proves how much it needs its gracious, merciful and redeeming Lord. Like Peter by the lakeside being given three chances to reverse the three denials he made on Maundy Thursday, the church is constantly humbled by the way God in Christ turns its failures into the Spirit's opportunities, and like the disciples on the Emmaus road finds its doubt and despair transformed by the strangers God sends its way.

Pascal was right. 'If' really is the most important word in history. The whole of the church's faith, the future of the universe and the meaning of all things hangs on that tiny little word. If Christ is risen, we can live life with angelic joy, because death is the gate of heaven, sin will be turned into grace and evil has no lasting power over us. Whether we live or die, God is with us and will never let us go. We live our lives in the strength, and the hope, and the promise, and the wonder, of that tiny, momentous, 'if'.

But on this day, on Easter Day, we go to the tomb with Mary, we hear the good shepherd speaking our name, we turn from the place of darkness and despair and destruction and death to the Lord of light and life and laughter and love. We see the stone of that little word 'if' rolled away, we look into the face of our creator and redeemer, and we gently mouth the three short words that change everything: Christ is risen.

Primal scream

However comfortable your life, however secure your relationships, however deeply you know you're loved, however stable your health, however strong your faith, there are, at bottom, two primal fears that stalk each one of us. The first fear shouts. It claims that there is, finally, no deep logic at work in the universe – that all attempts to find meaning and purpose are in the end arbitrary. There is no guiding divine hand at work at the beginning, middle or end of all things, There is no ultimate truth and the whole of existence is either a joke or an accident. The second fear is subtly different. It whispers. It whispers that there is indeed a logic, purpose, meaning, truth in the universe: but that this ultimate orientation, this God as we conventionally call it, has an interest, attention or judgement that lies elsewhere, and is not, in the end, on our side.

Imagine you've been diagnosed with a terminal illness. Part of you is rational: you say, 'I know everyone dies. Why should I expect to live longer than anyone else?' Another part is emotional: you say, 'I can't bear to think of my children trying to cope without me. I can't face the prospect of not existing, all my life coming to nothing.' Another part of you is desperate: 'Don't let this happen! There must be a cure! I'll try anything!' These all shout into the abyss of meaninglessness. But there's also the whisper into the heart of cruelty: 'God, why are you punishing me? Do I not matter to you, after all? Have you forgotten me? Do you have some kind of plan to make me suffer?'

Or imagine that you long to find a person with whom to share your life. Part of you asks the shouty question – 'Why won't it happen for me like I see it happening to others?' Or maybe it becomes self-blame – 'Is there something wrong with me?' Or possibly cynicism – 'There's no point and in any case you can't trust people and love's an illusion anyway – the world's just full of people who haven't yet found that out.' But at the back of your head there's often the whispering question, saying maybe you're being singled out for isolation: 'Is God punishing me?' And there's sometimes a sense of persecution or absurdity: 'There must be some conspiracy that sends me all the heartless and the selfish ones.' 'Is God laughing out loud that I only fall for the ones that never look at me?'

Such experiences reveal these two primal fears: the shout that there's no God, no truth, no meaning; and the whisper that there is a purpose, there is a logic – but that it's set against me.

The gospels present us with the figure of Jesus. Think for a moment about how he appears when set against these two primal fears. There's the fear that life is meaningless – that there's no purpose to anything. Jesus lives a life that is beautiful because it's generous, gentle and sacrificial, a life that's challenging because it's full of controversy, suffering and courage, but also a life that's compelling because it's inviting, intriguing and demanding. Above all he tells a story that includes his life, then the life of Israel, then the life of the church and the whole world, and all within the story of God. He doesn't prove anything, but he thrills and entices and questions and empowers so much that we want to walk with him to Jerusalem, to Galilee, to the kingdom of heaven.

Then there's the fear that God is against us. Jesus comes to Israel, a people living under occupation, who fear that God's turned against them; and every gesture he makes, in healing lepers, speaking with and touching shunned women, forgiving and calling tax-collectors, denouncing scribes – it all proclaims that God is on our side, God has no bone to pick with us, God is like a shepherd who travels to the furthest corner of the countryside to retrieve the lost sheep, like a father who pines every day for the return of his lost son, like a woman who searches high and low for a lost coin. You could say the whole of the gospels are written to address these two primal fears and to say, yes, there is an almighty God, but yes, that almighty God is on our side and is made not of petulance but of mercy, not of judgement but of grace.

But where's the proof? Thus far Christians are simply those who, given the choice between meaning and meaninglessness, choose the former, and given the choice between a God of vindictiveness and a God of grace, choose the latter. One could easily say that's just a choice. And that primal fear still shouts or whispers in the background, saying faith is just a whistling in the wind.

And that brings us to Holy Week. Because Holy Week refers to the eight days in which Jesus addresses the depth of these two primal fears comprehensively, agonisingly and conclusively. On Good Friday Jesus faces the duplicity of the authorities, the betrayal of Judas, the denial of Peter, the cowardice of Pilate, the cruelty of the soldiers, the ridicule of the crowds, the agony of the nails, the horror of suffocation, the humiliation of nakedness and – more than all the rest put together – the indescribable primal fear of being forsaken by the Father. When you weigh all of these dimensions up, what you see is that Good Friday is so important because it answers that second, whispering fear: is God truly on our side? Well, if what Jesus goes through on Good Friday doesn't persuade us that God is on our side, nothing will. Jesus goes through every level of physical, emotional, relational, psychological and cosmic agony. Why? Because he is the embodiment of God's determination never to be except to be with us.

It's not that God is some faraway deity who for unknown reasons fixates on humankind and decides to identify with us until it all gets too costly. It's that we are in God's DNA – God had us in mind when the universe began, God always meant to be with us in Jesus, and our perfidy, fecklessness and folly weren't going to alter that. God has no other plan than the plan to be with us. Christmas embodies that: Good Friday proves it.

But that still leaves one primal fear hanging. The shouty one. Jesus may be offering us something beautiful, showing us something wonderful, demonstrating something good, affirming us more profoundly than any casual remark or kind gift. But that could be no more than a glorious gesture, if ultimately it comes out of a commitment that's founded on hope not sureness, idealism not reality, shifting sands of fantasy not solid rock of truth. So where do we go looking for that truth? We go to the biggest rival of all, the deepest chasm of all – the unavoidable prospect of death. And here we come face to face with the most significant moment in history. Peter and the Beloved Disciple see the empty tomb and the folded grave clothes. That evening in the upper room the eleven disciples feel the breath of God. A week later, Thomas touches the wounds in the Lord's hands and side. Right here, right now, Mary Magdalene hears Jesus calling her name. 'Mary'. The name of the one whose womb brought Jesus to birth. The name of the one who, beside the tomb, sees Jesus come to new birth.

'Mary.' That one word tells her that the cross was not a beautiful failure; that the one who is on her side is not defeated by horror or pain or betrayal or duplicity or denial or agony or forsakenness; that there's ultimately no difference between the love that lays its life down for us and the power that brings that life back to us. That power, in the blood-drenched hands of her crucified Lord, is so gentle that it waits for her to make her own journey, so patient that it understands her confusion, so tender that it simply calls her by name. But it speaks to her from the other side of fear, from a deeper place than her primal anxiety, with a confidence that can wait as long as it takes and a kindness that lets her discover in her own way.

We have two primal fears: that there's no God, or that there is a God but it's a God who's against us. On Good Friday we meet a God who's utterly with us, right down to the agony and horror of death and hell. On Easter Day, we meet a tender, gentle, patient presence that turns out to have met us from the other side of fear, death, separation and primal despair. Look at those hands. Look at that face. Hear those words. Feel a love that death cannot destroy. A love where truth and power meet. A love that cannot be kept down. A power that's forever. And an eternal truth that knows your name.

Three whispers

Thirty-five years ago, I was playing in a rugby game when I got the heel of a boot in my neck. A few hours later I could hardly breathe and a hospital doctor did a tracheotomy, which meant that for the next two weeks air came in and out through my throat. The blood went over my vocal cords and it seemed I wouldn't be able to speak properly again. In the event the two main casualties were my singing voice and my ability to shout. You won't ever hear me shout because I can't. So I had to learn a different way to impose my authority. (What authority? I hear you say.) Eventually I worked it out. The way to be heard isn't to shout. It's to whisper.

There are several kinds of occasions when we whisper. One is when we're frightened. I remember years ago coming back to the flat where I lived and finding the door open. I should have been strong and manly but I wasn't. I was whispering to see if my companion and I could work out whether there were burglars in the flat and which room they were in. Even when we found no burglar it was hard to speak again in a normal voice. Another time we whisper is when we're keeping a secret. We're at the back of class and like all school pupils we believe that teachers can't hear what's being whispered at more than twelve feet away. We're digging our way out of the prisoner of war camp, and we whisper to the person removing the earth from the tunnel. Best of all is when we're intimate with someone special: we're sharing touch and darkness and we're saying something we've never told anyone before. It's a moment of discovery, revelation, disclosure, and the whisper makes it precious, trustful and true.

I want to talk about three whispers: three whispers that tell the whole story of everything. You can't tell much that matters by shouting, but you can explore the whole mystery of everything in three whispers. Huddle close, to make sure you can hear. It's time to whisper the whole mystery of everything. Here we go.

We didn't choose to be born, any of us. Yet at some moment in our childhood, each of us realized that we were alive. It struck us one moment, or dawned on us gradually, that we were in the midst of an astonishing, beautiful, exhilarating drama, which careered on largely without our will or assistance. That drama wasn't just a spectacle; we got to play a role in it; in fact, we had as much chance as anyone to play a part. That drama hadn't always been: once it had not been, and even more pressing, once we had not been; but now we are. That was the moment, that instant in our childhood, when we became aware of life.

But one night we looked into the sky and saw a gazillion stars, most of which probably burnt out trillions of years ago but whose light we're only now seeing; and we realized that this life – our life, all life – is just a whisper in the cacophony of the universe. We're a tiny speck in the story of everything. From across the universe we're even tinier than the most minuscule star is to us. But that whisper is the whisper on which everything we know depends. We're a whisper; a tiny one. It doesn't matter how quiet a whisper is: what matters is the words it says. And the whisper that says the word 'Life' is precious beyond any blast of sound. It's a whisper that communicates indescribable energy, creativity, vigour, joy. The elixir of life.

But a little bit later in our childhood we realize that life isn't the only thing going on. There's something that comes to everyone, to everything, that takes the joy out of life. As you become a teenager, you realize that everyone only deals with it by pretending it isn't there. But it infiltrates every life, and every aspect of life, with its menace and destruction. On the rugby field that day 35 years ago, I rejoiced in the first whisper – the whisper of life, running, kicking, tackling, passing, enjoying, exulting. But in the hospital that night I glimpsed in the registrar's worried face and the nurses' anxious attentions the spectre of a second whisper: death. I came suddenly, unexpectedly, very close to death. Death is what we could call the second whisper. It's a mystery, just as deep and impenetrable as life. Why is there life? We don't usually ask the question, but we're glad there is. We laugh at the question, because everything we can imagine depends on there being life. But if there's life, why is there death? It's unthinkable, intolerable, unjust. Does the second whisper cancel out the first whisper – shout it down, dismantle and discredit it? What's the point of the first whisper if we have to face the second whisper? How do we find our way out of the everlasting wrestle between life and death? Do we fear, deep down, that death eventually wins, every time? Is that why we whisper – because we don't want to admit it, we try to keep the secret, don't want anyone else to know?

Tucked away near the middle of the Old Testament, half-way through the last chapter of one of its most neglected books, just where no one's going to look for them, are the most important words in the Bible. They're the most important because they break open this perpetual arm-wrestle between life and death. Set me as a seal upon your heart, as a seal upon your arm; for love is strong as death. Those five words are the epicentre of the Bible: *love is strong as death*. There's only one way to say them and that's to whisper them. Death thinks it's got the better of life – it will always win in the end. It will destroy, dismantle and discredit everything, and turn it to dust. But there's something death hasn't bargained for. And that's love. And when we discover love we find the answers to our two greatest questions. Why is there life? Because of love. Love is what life was created for. Will life outlast death? No – but love will. Death can't drown love. Many floods can't quench its fire.

However happy the happiest day of your life, there's a sadness lurking in the shadows. It's the sadness of that second whisper. You can love someone but that doesn't mean he doesn't die. Someone can love you, but that doesn't always mean her love for you won't die. You can work for 30 years to build up a business, but that doesn't mean a pandemic can't bring it crashing down. You can love a grandparent your whole life but you can watch a virus tear her away from you in just a few days.

When Mary Magdalene goes to the tomb on the morning of the first Easter Day, she knows more than anyone about the first whisper – because she's seen life like no one's known it before: she's met Jesus, she's watched him heal the leper and raise the dead, she's heard him speak the words of eternal life. But she also knows more than anyone about the second whisper, because she's seen this man who embodied everything life could mean nailed to a cross, tortured, betrayed, denied, rejected. She's seen how everything in life can be turned into merciless death. Perhaps more than anyone in history, on that first Easter morning she's bewildered by the contrast between life and death, the first whisper and the second – and she goes to the tomb weighing one with the other in her mind and heart and soul.

What she finds there is the most important discovery ever made. It's the discovery that makes sense of all the glorious mysteries of life and the desultory mysteries of death. She discovers there's a third mystery. She discovers the central claim of the Christian faith: love is stronger than death. What she discovers is resurrection. This is the mystery that unravels the mystery of life and death. Resurrection is the way, the only way, human beings reach out from the constraints of life and touch forever. And even more wonderfully resurrection is the way forever reaches out from beyond death and touches us with its truth.

The day I left that hospital 35 years ago I discovered there was something more powerful than shouting or even singing. I learned how to whisper. And since then, I've discovered that you can shout about resurrection and it can be impressive and you can sing about resurrection and it can be beautiful. But for the things that matter most in our lives, the things we dare to believe and fear to say out loud, the most precious way to put those things into words is to whisper.

We know life is short and fragile; we know death is bleak and cruel. But there's a third whisper, which is the reason that life was created and the only thing stronger than death. That whisper is resurrection, and to be a Christian is to whisper it together, in the dawn of the day, in the glow of the evening, in the darkness of the night, every day, so that when life is over and death has done its worst, that whisper will still be rustling and will speak louder than any scream or shout. It's a whisper that may mean danger, may require secrecy, but will in the end be the most intimate and joyful truth we share with the one who made life and transcended death. That whisper, which hitherto has always said the one word, 'resurrection', will finally turn into the only word that can match it, the word that makes it irresistible, the word that dismantles death and transcends mortality. That word can't be shouted or screamed but can only be whispered softly, because it's the secret at the heart of the universe, the secret beyond life and death, the secret of God and us. That word is 'forever'.

Still together

A while ago a friend said to me, 'It must be tough being a vicar at Easter.' I said, 'Why? It's the most inspiring time of the whole year. There's forgiveness and eternal life, and if you want something softer, there's bunnies and chocolate eggs. What's not to like?' He said, 'Yeah. *You* think that. But the truth is, everyone still prefers Christmas.'

It set me thinking. There are two kinds of perfection. There's first-day perfection, straight-out-of-the-wrapping paper, no-smudge-marks, untarnished perfection. And there's rescued-from-the-scrapheap, polished-from-accumulated-dust, saved-from-the-abyss perfection.

What's wrong with the first-day kind of perfection? I'll tell you: it has no story. In fact, story's the enemy of that sort of perfection. If you're starting with perfection, every develop-ment of the narrative introduces problems and failures and disappointments. If you think about our frustration with life, it's mostly that life isn't first-day perfection. It isn't always fair, it isn't always happy, it isn't always easy, it isn't always fun, it isn't always reliable, it isn't always beautiful. It isn't always done for us. It isn't Christmas every day, with the stars aligned, the kings come to give us a standing ovation, the shepherds singing a merry tune and a gorgeous baby in our arms. It's not hard to believe in God at Christmas.

It's much tougher to believe in God at Easter. Think of the 48 hours leading up to Easter. You've got the two hardest things in the world to come to terms with. One is the ghastly, undeniable, merciless horror of human cruelty and violence. The passion story is riddled with it: conspiracy, denial, betrayal, desertion, assault, imprisonment, torture, agony, mockery, humiliation, horror. The other is the sheer physicality and unutterable tragedy of death. All the suffering of Christ's passion would be redeem-able if it didn't end in death.

This is the big question at the heart of all things: is love stronger than sin and death? We're so mesmerized by the per-vasiveness of sin and the finality of death that we struggle to believe it. We look at the Easter story and our defences kick in and we say, 'It's wish fulfilment, it's groupthink, it's mass delusion. There's no way this could happen.'

In the end, all of us have to choose, in parenthood, in mar-riage or partnership, in work, in life, whether to continue to perpetuate the fantasy of the first day, the story without a story, the notion that things won't change but can be perpetually per-fect – or whether to inhabit the reality of the real story, which has ups and downs, pain and joy, separation and togetherness, the mundane and the wonderful. The Christian faith is the second kind of story. The good news is, the story's still going, even after Good Friday. Nothing can end the story. That's what we discover at Easter.

At the heart of Japanese culture is the practice of kintsugi. Kintsugi makes a virtue of breakages in pottery, which it highlights using gold lacquer. Instead of trying to hide the repair and pretend the pot is good as new, kintsugi makes the repair the most noticeable feature of the pot. Every one of us has to face the breakage of our perfect story. Every one of us knows the impulse to hide the damage. Easter doesn't pretend to be a perfect story. The risen Jesus has the scars of the nails. This is a real story, not a fantasy of unblemished perfection.

Twenty-five years ago, the Canadian singer-songwriter Shania Twain sought words of encouragement for her producer-husband, Mutt Lange. When they got together in 1993, nobody gave their marriage a chance. Twain wrote a song called 'You're still the one' that acknowledged the sentiments of their many critics. She's well aware what people are saying – 'You'll never make it.' She recognizes the challenges, the long road, and the satisfaction of proving everyone wrong: there's nothing better than beating the odds together. But the heart of the song isn't putting two fingers up to their doubters. It's the sense of quiet resilience, gentle momentum, that they've got something few will ever understand and perhaps even they themselves will never fully comprehend. Nothing in the end compares to what they find in one another – this is the person each still runs to, belongs to, wants to be with always. And then the most moving words, which sum up the whole song: she draws attention to the two of them, holding on, and sings, 'We're *still together, still going strong.*'

Christmas isn't a pottery bowl all wrapped up and designed never to be used. It really is the beginning of a story, a story that will inevitably have some breakages and repairs. God doesn't seem to want unblemished perfection with us – God wants real life, genuine relationship, in which trust is put in jeopardy, patience is strained, understanding is confused and forgiveness is essential.

None of this is there at Christmas – it all lies ahead. When people say, 'Expectation is better than experience', they're saying reality always spoils it; they're hankering after perfection without a story. But Easter tells us God being with us is a real story, with serious imperfections. God's relationship with us undergoes the very worst strains any relationship ever could: the coldness of disloyalty, duplicity, desertion and denial, and the ultimate separation of death. Here's the question at the end of Good Friday: is isolation our final fate? If there is a God, will that God never again be in relationship with us, because we have, in the most unequivocal terms, expunged all desire for such relationship from our presence? And left to ourselves, is there nothing to wait for but the eventual dismantling of all human relationship through sin and our utter isolation through death and oblivion? In the face of this bleakness, Easter has a quiet but totally wonderful response. Jesus reminds Mary in the garden that the doubters said they wouldn't make it. Mary replies to Jesus that he's still the one she runs to, belongs to, wants to be with always. She was muttering it under her breath, fighting back tears of desolation on her way to the tomb. Now she's laughing as she sings it through tears of joy with Jesus standing in front of her.

This isn't simply about a man and a woman in a garden, though that's a nice nod to the Garden of Eden story right back at the start of the Bible – back at the time the story started to get complicated and the relationship departed from its pristine beginnings. This is a story about God and humanity. The relationship's gone through the worst imaginable damage and destruction. But here we are, in the garden on Easter morning, and Jesus and Mary are singing, 'They said, "I bet they'll never make it." But just look at us holding on. We're still together, still going strong.'

This is the wonder of Easter. It's not the end of sin: sin seems to be still very much around us. It's not the end of death: death seems to be very much present. As it happens. Shania Twain and Mutt Lange didn't make it either. They split up ten years after writing the song. In real stories, no happy endings are guaranteed. But the gospel has always been proclaimed by fragile prophets. The song 'You're still the one' lives long beyond its authors' capacity to embody it and points to the deepest truth of Easter. In this eternal image of Mary and Jesus in the garden we have the conclusive statement that God and humanity are ultimately inseparable. There's no future for God that's not wrapped up in humanity, and there's no destiny for humanity outside the hands and the arms of God.

We're surrounded by doubters without and suspicion and mistrust within. Plenty of people are available to say we'll never make it. We're distressed at the complexity of life and the way it's never pure and seldom simple, and we're perplexed that it's always lived on the edge of death. But Easter shows us that there's only one thing that matters. And that is, we're never alone. There's no humanity that's not at the heart of God. There's no God that's not utterly wrapped up in humanity. Everything rests on that word 'together'. Still together. This isn't a fantasy where pottery never breaks. It's a real story, where terrible things happen, but those terrible things are not the end of the story – they just show the story's true. But we're still holding on. We're *still together, still going strong.*

God and humanity: still together. Still going strong. On Easter Day. Today. Every day. And forever.